THE 21-DAY
HEALTHY
SMOOTHIE
PLAN

THE 21-DAY HEALTHY SMOOTHIE PLAN

Invigorating Smoothies & Daily Support
for Wellness & Weight Loss

BY JENNIFER KOSLO, RD

SONOMA
PRESS

CONTENTS

BUILDING HEALTHY HABITS

Whether you're looking to slim down, kick your health up a notch, or just include more fruits and vegetables in your daily diet, you don't need to hire a personal chef or spend hours in the kitchen—all you need is a blender. Smoothies are ideal for quick, healthy, and totally delicious meals on the go. You can give your body what it needs and cut out unhealthy foods from your diet. The number of healthy smoothie combinations is endless! By following the plan outlined in this book, you will learn how to put together nutrient-dense ingredients and make a satisfying meal that will nourish your body, reduce cravings, and keep you feeling full and energized for hours.

Smoothies are ideal for quick, healthy, and totally delicious meals on the go.

Making smoothies is quick and convenient, and they easily fit into people's busy lifestyles. Building healthy habits takes inner motivation and a desire to change, coupled with a plan that includes realistic goals. *The 21-Day Healthy Smoothie Plan* will guide you step-by-step and educate you about these very important details:

* What constitutes a healthy smoothie (as opposed to an indulgent milk shake)
* How to blend to perfection
* Which equipment to use
* What to do when things don't turn out quite as they should

By the end of the plan, you'll be hooked on this healthy habit.

PART 1
GETTING STARTED

CHAPTER 1

BLEND, BABY, BLEND

Imagine being able to get more than half of your recommended intake of fruits, vegetables, good fats, fiber, and protein in one healthy meal that requires minimal prep and cleanup. The good news is that not only can you do this by learning how to make smoothies, but you can also make ones that taste delicious and that your body will crave!

When you have a good blender and quality ingredients, making a delicious, healthy smoothie is a snap. Smoothies are made from whole-some foods, and by making it yourself, you know exactly what is in it—no hidden junk—and you control the calorie content. A homemade smoothie is an excellent solution for the following:

- Breakfast on the go
- Post-workout meals
- Hearty snacks
- Lunch or dinner replacements

Do you want to overhaul your eating habits? Ready to shift to a diet with more fresh fruits and vegetables and fewer processed foods? Was that a "yes"? Well, reading the following lists just might convince you to develop a daily habit of making smoothies. What an excellent investment in your health!

10 REASONS TO LOVE SMOOTHIES

You may be wondering why so many people drink smoothies on a regular basis. They've become a bit of a buzz, suitable for everyone from babies to grannies. Smoothies are leading the way to optimal health and can be a cornerstone for an overall diet and nutrition makeover. After reading the following list, you'll know why making a habit of drinking healthy smoothies on a daily basis is an outstanding investment in your health.

1 **Improve your morning routine.** Smoothies are one of the fastest meals on the planet, especially if you invest a little bit of time in properly prepping your ingredients. By just tossing your ingredients in a blender and waiting for the blades to do their magic, you'll have a nutritious, sumptuous meal-in-a-glass at the ready any time of day. Smoothies make particularly good breakfast options for those who are always rushing out the door without having had a solid meal.

2 **Break up with the drive-thru.** Business lunches, soccer practice, PTA meetings—food is everywhere, and much of it is out of your control. It's easy to let one bad decision lead to others, and before you know it, your car is going through the drive-thru window on the way home from a long day. Having a smoothie each day means that you are in control of at least one of your meals. Why not make it a family affair and ensure that everyone has at least one balanced meal? Drinking a filling smoothie can remove the temptation of indulging in empty calories, and you won't have to go searching for other foods to fulfill your nutritional requirements.

3 **Disguise the spinach.** While it may not taste like candy, spinach is a green smoothie secret ingredient, and giving it a try will take your nutrition to the next level. Spinach is low in calories and high in antioxidants, vitamins, minerals, and fiber. It has a mild flavor and can easily be dominated by strongly flavored fruits and additives like nut butters. Smoothies make a great vehicle for hiding other ingredients too like flaxseed, beets, green soybeans, and even broccoli.

4 **Add versatility.** One of the best things about smoothies is that you can tailor them to your unique nutritional needs. Healthy smoothies are dense in nutrients and contain a good mix of protein, carbohydrates, and healthy fats. You can modify the types and amounts of ingredients and the calorie count to create a pre- or post-workout smoothie or a smoothie customized to meet your nutritional

requirements for breakfast, lunch, dinner, or as a snack. No two smoothies are exactly the same!

5 **Sneak fruits and vegetables into your kids' diets.** If your kids' favorite vegetables are French fries and ketchup, you know all too well the challenge of incorporating healthier foods. Blending fruit with milk, yogurt, and nut butters can suddenly turn foods your kids won't eat into something yummy! Kid-friendly smoothies can be made in five minutes or less and are a great way to ensure your kids are getting the nutrients their growing bodies need. Get the kids involved by letting them choose ingredients they like and help with the process of making the smoothies. Pour your kid-friendly smoothies into a thermos for those mornings when you're rushing out the door, or make smoothie pops by pouring them into popsicle molds and putting them in the freezer.

6 **Save money.** Homemade smoothies are cheap. Buying a healthy breakfast or lunch can cost you close to $10, and buying smoothies at a juice bar can set you back as much as $6 a glass. Once you stock your pantry, making a smoothie at home by combining fruits and vegetables will cost you half as much or even less. Frozen fruits and vegetables are some of the most economical options available, and they are just as nutritious as fresh produce—plus, you don't have to worry about them spoiling. So load up your grocery bag with nutritious smoothie ingredients and save yourself some money.

7 **Develop an easy, daily habit.** Replacing a meal each day with a smoothie is an easy habit to develop—much simpler than that marathon you keep meaning to train for and run. Developing a new habit takes practice, the right cues, and the tools you need to be successful. By having your ingredients prepped and cues like a post-it note on your bathroom mirror, you can gradually build a new healthy habit. The fact that smoothies are delicious will make it much more likely that you'll be successful.

8 **Have some fun!** With the right blender and some basic know-how, you may find that making smoothies brings out your creative side. Mixing and matching various ingredients may have you feeling like a modern-day alchemist, noting characteristics, flavors, and textures. Before you know it, you may be posting original recipes online. Loads of people love making smoothies, so why not join the fun?

9 **Learn a lot about nutrition.** Good fats, bad fats, fiber, protein, vitamins, minerals, antioxidants, probiotics—by learning what constitutes a healthy smoothie, you'll educate yourself on how to follow a healthy diet. By taking note of serving sizes, you'll see how your diet compares to recommendations and what changes you may want to make. You'll also feel the difference in your energy levels and digestion between a diet high in processed foods and one where whole fresh foods take center stage. Then when the blender isn't around, you'll feel more confident in your food choices.

10 **Simplify your food decisions.** When you make a nutritious smoothie every day, you'll simplify your food decisions. You may also find that you think about food less. Because food is literally everywhere in our society, we're faced with hundreds of food decisions each day. A typical grocery store has upward of 30,000 different items! If you start your day off with a healthy smoothie containing good fats, adequate protein, complex carbohydrates, and enough calories, your cravings will decrease dramatically, simplifying your food decisions.

BLENDED BENEFITS

Smoothies are a great way to get in a few servings of fruits, vegetables, healthy omega-3 fats, fiber, and most importantly, phytochemicals. So aside from being a delicious meal, what health benefits can a well-made smoothie offer? The following list highlights a few of the more noteworthy ways in which smoothies can improve your health and well-being.

Boost beautiful and healthy hair, skin, and nails. By loading up your smoothie with nutrient-dense ingredients, you will be supplying your body with the raw materials it needs to grow healthier hair and keep your skin and nails healthy. Biotin is a water-soluble B vitamin that is known for its role in promoting healthy hair growth and protecting against dryness. Smoothie ingredients where biotin can be found include bananas, berries, peanut butter, sunflower seeds, oatmeal, avocados, almonds, and Swiss chard. Other essential skin, hair, and nail nutrients include folic acid, vitamin C, lutein, vitamin D, omega-3 fats, and essential amino acids. Good sources include nondairy milks and yogurts, leafy greens, nuts (especially walnuts) and seeds, and most fruits and vegetables.

Blending vs. Juicing

So what's the difference between blending and juicing? A juicer extracts vitamins and minerals from fruits and vegetables, leaving the fiber behind. The lack of fiber makes it easy to consume large amounts of fruits and vegetables in one drink. Blending, however, breaks up the fiber in fruits and vegetables so it is easier to digest, but leaves it in the drink so you get the same benefits you would if you ate whole fruits and vegetables. While each type of drink has its benefits, it is easy to overdo it on natural sugars when you juice, and juices tend to be digested superfast so they aren't meant to be meal replacements. Juicing requires a juicer that can remove the pulp from fruits and vegetables, and you can expect to spend about $200 for a quality piece of equipment. If you are thinking about juicing, check out these 10 wonderful books:

- *Best Green Drinks Ever: Boost Your Juice with Antioxidants, Protein and More* by Katrine Van Wyk

- *The Big Book of Juices: More Than 400 Natural Blends for Health and Vitality Every Day* by Natalie Savona

- *The Everything Juicing Book: All You Need to Create Delicious Juices for Optimum Health* by Carole Jacobs

- *The Healthy Green Drink Diet: Advice and Recipes to Energize, Alkalize, Lose Weight, and Feel Great* by Jason Manheim

- *The Juice Cleanse Reset Diet: 7 Days to Transform Your Body for Increased Energy, Glowing Skin, and a Slimmer Waistline* by Lori Kenyon Farley and Marra St. Clair

- *The Juice Generation: 100 Recipes for Fresh Juices and Superfood Smoothies* by Eric Helms with Amely Greevan

- *The Juicing Bible* by Pat Crocker

- *Juicing Recipes for Vitality and Health* by Drew Canole

- *The Reboot with Joe Juice Diet: Lose Weight, Get Healthy, and Feel Amazing* by Joe Cross

- *Superfood Juices: 100 Delicious, Energizing & Nutrient-Dense Recipes* by Julie Morris

Rival the quality and cost of multivitamins. Vitamin and mineral supplements are not regulated by the Food and Drug Administration, nor are they tested for safety or efficacy before they are put on the market. Supplements can contain much more or much less of the ingredients listed on the supplements fact panel, and there is no way for you to know. Save yourself some money, and use your supplement cash for buying organic fresh and frozen fruits and vegetables to use in your smoothies.

Enhance sleep. Tart cherries are one of the only natural food sources of melatonin, the chemical that controls the body's internal clock to regulate sleep. Preliminary research published in the *Journal of Medicinal Food* (2010) has found that tart cherry juice has a modest, beneficial effect on sleep in adults with insomnia. Bananas, a good source of the natural muscle relaxants potassium and magnesium, are another sleep promoter. Bananas also contain the amino acid L-tryptophan, which gets converted to serotonin, a relaxing neurotransmitter, and to melatonin. Oats, a complex carbohydrate, can ease you into sleep by promoting the release of serotonin and tryptophan, making them a good addition to an evening smoothie. Using chamomile tea as the liquid in your smoothie can also promote a restful night's sleep.

Detoxify your body. You can help your body's natural detoxifying abilities by creating smoothies that contain naturally cleansing ingredients. Doing so will promote the release of water, increase circulation, and keep your kidneys and liver healthy. In addition to including purified water as your liquid, there are a number of delicious ingredients you can use in your daily smoothie to aid your body's natural processes. Detoxifying smoothie ingredients include lemons, limes, watermelons, cranberries, celery, cucumbers, dandelion greens, kale, apples, avocados, beets, pineapples, cilantro, fennel, ginger, and parsley, to name a few.

Fight diseases. A recent study published in the *American Journal of Epidemiology* investigated the relationship between fruit and vegetable consumption and mortality in 451,151 participants from 10 countries. The results showed that consumption of fruits and vegetables was inversely associated with all-cause mortality. In other words, eat your fruits and veggies to live longer and reduce your chances of developing chronic diseases.

Lose weight more easily. If you are trying to lose weight, then blending up a nutrient-dense smoothie will be your secret weapon. The reason smoothies are such great weight loss tools is because you are in control of the ingredients and the calorie content. It's easy to learn how to assemble a low-calorie, nutritionally balanced smoothie that will keep you full for hours. You can also include add-ins that can increase your metabolic rate and balance your blood sugar. Green tea has compounds that can stimulate metabolism, avocados can increase satiety, chia seeds are full of fiber, and cinnamon can help balance blood sugar levels. If you are the daring type, adding a dash of cayenne, which contains the compound capsaicin, can help curb your appetite.

Recover from exercise. One of the best things about smoothies is that you can tailor the ingredients to your individual nutrient needs and to specific meals or snacks. Instead of buying an expensive powdered protein drink for a post-workout meal, blend up one of the recipes in this book. Contrary to popular belief, you don't need gobs of protein to build muscle. Instead, you need healthy carbohydrates, moderate protein, and healthy fats to replace muscle fuel and to repair and build tissue.

Get your daily allowance of fruits and vegetables. Meeting the recommended intake for fruits and vegetables can be a challenge. By blending two or more servings of each into your daily smoothie, you can ensure that you are on your way to meeting your nutritional goals.

Hydrate yourself. Did you know that high-water fruits and vegetables like celery and watermelon count toward your daily water requirements? Water constitutes about 60 percent of an adult's body weight, and adequate water is essential for carrying nutrients and wastes throughout the body, maintaining blood volume, regulating body temperature, and keeping our body processes running smoothly. By drinking one healthy smoothie each day, you'll hydrate your body and contribute to your daily fluid requirements.

Improve digestion. Smoothie ingredients are unprocessed, and the fruit and vegetable contents are full of fiber, vitamins, minerals, and antioxidants, which are readily absorbed by your body. Regular consumption of fiber is essential to one's health, and most people don't get enough in their diets, which can result in poor digestion and constipation. Just one healthy smoothie a day can help you meet at least half of the daily recommended intake of 25 to 35 grams of dietary fiber and keep your digestive system running efficiently.

Support your immune system. Fruits, vegetables, and nuts are full of phytochemicals, antioxidants, vitamins, minerals, and healthy fats, all of which are needed to keep your immune system strong. Nutrients that are of particular importance for immunity include vitamins A, B_2, B_6, C, D, and E and the minerals selenium and zinc. Ingredients that you can add to your smoothie for more immune support include probiotics, in the form of cultured soy, coconut yogurt, or kefir; blueberries; cherries; Goji berries; pumpkin; nuts and seeds; and green tea.

Lessen cravings for junk food. When you start your day off with a nutrient-dense smoothie that contains enough calories and some healthy fats, you will find that your cravings for unhealthy fatty foods, especially in the evening, will decrease dramatically. Trying to limit calories or eliminate fat entirely from your diet will just backfire. Doing so may trigger overeating or, even worse, bingeing.

Extend energy and balance blood sugar. With the right mix of ingredients, smoothies can regulate your appetite and keep your blood sugar steady so you don't experience highs and lows during the day. Meals that contain protein, healthy fats, complex carbohydrates, and no refined sugars provide steady fuel to your brain and working muscles, keep your blood sugar balanced, and keep your mood even. Eliminating carbohydrates or fat or restricting calories can lead to low energy, mood swings, fatigue, and low blood sugar. The recipes in this book are all nutritionally balanced and will give you energy to fuel your busy day.

Reach your personal health goals. Whether you are trying to lose weight; increase your intake of fruits and vegetables, healthy fats, or fiber; or decrease your intake of sodium, cholesterol, saturated fats, and refined sugars, smoothies can be tailored to meet your individual health goals. Packed with phytochemicals and nutrients, a smoothie a day can kick the quality of your diet up a notch or two.

Befriending Your Freezer

The nutrient content of frozen fruits and vegetables is comparable to fresh produce and, in some cases, it may even be higher. Produce that is frozen is processed immediately after harvesting, so nutrient losses after picking are minimal. Depending on the food, freezing may actually preserve some of the nutrient value and even increase the availability of some nutrients to the body. Fresh fruits and vegetables can go bad in a couple of days, so using frozen varieties means less waste. Using frozen fruits and vegetables also saves time because you don't have to wash or cut anything. Stock your freezer so you can prepare nutritious smoothies year-round.

SMOOTHIE SNAFUS

Smoothies are a delicious and easy way to pack in loads of nutrients without having to break out any cookware, but the devil is in the details. A poorly constructed smoothie can be higher in calories, fat, and processed additives than a fast-food meal—increasing inflammation, spiking your blood sugar, and causing your waistline to expand. Here are some of the most common smoothie snafus.

You add too many nuts or too much nut butter. Almond, hazelnut, cashew, sunflower seed, walnut, peanut ... the list goes on. Just about every type of nut also has a nut butter that is commercially produced for sale. You can buy most nuts in bulk and get your own freshly ground nut butters at most health-food stores. The fat content of nuts and nut butters makes them unbelievably satisfying, and adding them to smoothies can make your drink thick, rich, and creamy. Unfortunately, overdoing the portion size of nuts and nut butters is one of the fastest ways to derail your healthy-eating plan. Stick to one-half or one-ounce portions of nuts and nut butters, which is approximately 100 to 200 calories, respectively. For whole nuts, that means just one-eighth of a cup or two tablespoons for a half-ounce portion and a quarter-cup for one ounce. For nut butters, one tablespoon is a half-ounce serving and more than enough for one drink. Spinach adds an amazing creamy texture, so moderate your portions of nuts and nut butters with an extra handful of this leafy vegetable.

You heard coconut oil is good for you. There is a lot of hype surrounding the health benefits of coconut oil, and the truth is there isn't enough scientific evidence to support all of the claims. While virgin coconut oil is high in medium-chain triglycerides, and it may have a beneficial effect on cholesterol, it is still a fat—period. One tablespoon of coconut oil has 120 calories with 14 grams of fat, 12 grams of which are saturated fat. For now, go easy on the serving size.

Fruit is nutritious, but you can have too much of a good thing. Fruits contain valuable vitamins, minerals, antioxidants, phytochemicals, and fiber, along with ample amounts of natural, simple sugars. Too much fruit and not enough protein or healthy fats, and your smoothie could end up giving you a not-so-pleasant sugar high followed by a sugar crash. To keep the fruit in your smoothies nutritious, stick to one or two servings of antioxidant-rich berries and cherries. Avoid fruit juices, which are calorie-dense and don't contain fiber.

There's no protein. The smoothie recipes in this book contain one or more servings of protein. Protein is the most satiating nutrient, which means it keeps you feeling full and satisfied. When you make a smoothie without a source of protein like hemp seeds, nuts, soy yogurt, or tofu, you may find yourself consuming a 300-calorie smoothie and so hungry in an hour that you eat three slices of pizza. Other types of protein that work well in smoothies are cooked beans and non-GMO plant-based protein powders like hemp, rice, pea, artichoke heart, and soy.

You include an avocado in every smoothie you make. Avocados are an amazingly healthy fruit. They are rich in heart-healthy monounsaturated fats and fiber, and there is scientific evidence that shows eating half of an avocado with a meal can keep you full longer. They also make smoothies rich and creamy. However, avocados are high in calories, so watch your portion sizes. One cup of avocado has about 234 calories, 21 grams of fat, 10 grams of fiber, and 3 grams of protein.

Miraculous Mixture?

Blending up a nutritious smoothie each day can help you with weight management and improve your overall nutrition. But one healthy smoothie a day can't undo an otherwise poor diet and a sedentary lifestyle. Strive to eat a diet that includes ample amounts of unprocessed fruits, vegetables, whole grains, healthy fats, and lean protein. Aim for five servings of vegetables and fruits each day and be active!

One serving of vegetables is one cup of raw leafy greens (about the size of a small fist), half of a cup of other vegetables, or half of a cup of 100 percent vegetable juice.

For fruits, a serving is equal to one medium fruit; half of a cup chopped, cooked, or canned fruit; or half of a cup of 100 percent fruit juice.

Physical activity goes hand in hand with eating healthfully. An ideal exercise program includes aerobic exercise, strength training, and flexibility exercises. A good goal is to work up to exercising four to six times per week for at least 30 to 60 minutes each time.

SMOOTHIE MANAGEMENT

Here's some guidance about what to keep in your smoothie and what to leave out.

SMOOTHIE BASES

- **Recommended:** Unsweetened almond milk, water, plain soy or coconut yogurt, purified water, tea, coffee, coconut water (in moderation)
- **Avoid:** Whole milk, store-bought juices

SMOOTHIE INGREDIENTS

- **Recommended:** Fresh or frozen fruit and vegetables, nuts, nut butters, seeds, oatmeal, high-quality protein powders, unsweetened cacao and cocoa
- **Avoid:** Ice cream, chocolate powders and syrups, sugar, Cool Whip, pudding mix, smoothie mixes out of a box

WHEN TO BLEND AND HOW TO STORE

While fresh is always best, a two-day-old green smoothie is still much better than a couple of Pop-Tarts or a drive-thru breakfast sandwich. If your goal is to improve your health and get more fruits and vegetables in your diet, nutritious smoothies will help you get there regardless of when you blend them. If your mornings are rushed and you don't have time to make smoothies fresh every morning, or if you don't want to wake the neighbors with the sound of your high-speed blender, you can make a batch on the weekend and freeze it for the week ahead. Something as simple as having a smoothie ready to go can make your life that much easier and your breakfast or lunch that much more nutritious.

Invest in freezable containers like Ball Plastic Freezer Jars or pick up some mason jars with lids for storing your smoothies. Quart-size mason jars are the perfect fit for most freezers, or choose eight-ounce jars for easy stacking. Set aside some time for prepping, then simply assemble and blend your smoothie and pour it into a freezable container. Make sure not to fill it to the rim because the smoothie will expand a bit while freezing. If you want to enjoy your smoothie for breakfast, pull it out of the freezer when you get out of bed and it will be drinkable by the time you drive to work. Having prepared frozen smoothies on hand also makes it easy to eat healthy on those nights when you get home from work and are too tired to cook.

Smoothies and Salads

By having a nutritious smoothie each day, you are set with one healthy meal. But what about the other meals? Two hamburgers and a smoothie does not a healthy diet make! Here's a good goal to aim for:

- One or two servings of vegetables

- A serving of lean protein (two to three ounces cooked)

- One portion of healthy fats (approximately one teaspoon of oil, one tablespoon of nuts, or one quarter of an avocado)

- A portion of slow-burning complex carbohydrates at your other meals

By choosing one of the recommended salads in this book as one of your other meals, you can rest assured that you are meeting many of your nutritional requirements each day. The suggested salads each include three or more servings of vegetables, are high in fiber, contain healthy fats, and have at least one serving of protein. They will keep you feeling full, energized, and satisfied, while holding your calories and cravings in check.

TROUBLESHOOTING GUIDE

Whenever you explore something new, there is a learning curve and a bit of experimentation involved. Don't get discouraged if your first couple of smoothies turn out less than perfect. Smoothie making isn't difficult. However, each blender is different, so you might have to tweak the recipes as you get to know your machine. The most important thing to remember is to have fun and enjoy experimenting. You know what they say: practice makes perfect!

MY SMOOTHIE IS . . . TOO CHUNKY OR GRAINY.

Solution: There could be several things at work here. First, you might not have blended long enough. Blenders vary greatly in their power, so it just might be that your blender isn't cutting it (literally), and you need to let it run for a bit longer to fully break down the ingredients. Some blenders simply can't handle raw veggies and fruits, in which case you might consider using a food processor to grind the fruits, veggies, and nuts before adding them to your smoothie. Another cause could be that you need to add a bit more liquid. Try adding an additional ¼ cup of your milk of choice and blend. You may need to repeat this a few times. Lastly, filling your blender jar to high might result in less than ideal blending, especially if you have an older or low-powered blender. Try blending your liquid, base, fresh fruit, and greens first, then add frozen fruit or ice and blend until smooth.

MY SMOOTHIE IS . . . TOO THIN.

Solution: There are a couple of ways to turn a watery smoothie into one that is thick and creamy. Try adding more frozen fruit, especially bananas, which can serve double duty by fixing the consistency, while masking any flavor snafus. If you have a high-powered blender, you can also try freezing a portion of your liquid ingredients in ice cube trays. Almond milk, coffee, and even yogurt can be frozen and added directly to the blender.

MY SMOOTHIE IS . . . TOO THICK.

Solution: To make your smoothie less thick without watering down the taste, add a bit more milk, half a cup at a time until you get the desired consistency. You can also add more water, but doing so may water down the taste. Another thing is to remember to load your blender container by putting the liquids in first, then soft fruits or vegetables, greens, and frozen fruits or vegetables and ice on top.

MY SMOOTHIE IS . . . TOO BITTER.

Solution: You accidently added arugula instead of spinach to your smoothie, and the result is a bitter-tasting drink. The best fix for a situation like this is to add banana, which in addition to being sweet, seems to neutralize bitter flavors. Pineapples and oranges both add lots of fruity sweetness, and strawberries are an especially good choice for green smoothies. Also try adding a bit of vanilla bean or vanilla extract, unsweetened cacao, or unsweetened cocoa powder. Keep a few plastic bags of frozen bananas and mango chunks on hand while you are testing different combinations. Another thing to remember is that baby greens are generally milder than mature greens. Also, your tastes change and adapt to new eating habits. Try working up to bitter greens by combining small amounts of them with spinach in your smoothie.

MY SMOOTHIE IS . . . TOO SWEET.

Solution: Fruits contribute their own natural sweetness so it shouldn't be necessary to add other sweeteners like honey or agave. But if you find your smoothie tastes too sugary or too syrupy, try adding just a touch of fresh lemon juice to cut down on the sweetness.

MY SMOOTHIE . . . ISN'T SWEET ENOUGH.

Solution: There are a number of ways to naturally sweeten a smoothie without adding sugar. By far the mother of all smoothie sweeteners is the Medjool date. Not just any date, this "king of dates" is super sweet and has a caramel-like taste that is compatible with just about any smoothie recipe. If you have a high-speed blender, just remove the pit and toss the date in. For low-powered blenders, try finely chopping it and soaking it in a little warm water before adding it to the liquid called for in the recipe. Blend it into a loose date paste before adding the rest of the

Tips for Type 2 Diabetics

If you have type 2 diabetes, you can enjoy all of the smoothies in this book as part of your healthy diabetic meal plan. The smoothies include enough protein, healthy fats, slow-burning carbohydrates, and fiber to meet the needs of most diabetics. However, if you currently have trouble managing your blood sugar levels, speak to a registered dietitian before replacing any of your meals with a healthy smoothie.

smoothie ingredients. Another great sweetening method is to use overripe bananas. Simply peel, cut, and freeze them in bags, and then pop them into the blender for added sweetness, as a thickener, and to mask bitter flavors.

MY SMOOTHIE . . . ISN'T CREAMY ENOUGH.

Solution: If your smoothie is lacking in the creaminess department, it may be that you need to adjust your liquid and solid ingredients to achieve the right texture. Some of the most magical sources of creaminess for smoothie heaven are nuts, nut butters, avocados, oatmeal (cooked or dry), cooked grains, nondairy yogurt, frozen bananas, and spinach.

MY SMOOTHIE IS . . . CHALKY TASTING.

Solution: If you decide to try out some protein powders in your smoothie, beware that powders are a tricky business, varying greatly in terms of ingredient quality, taste, and texture. Some powders add a chalky or grainy texture, while others add a bit of creaminess. You may want to start with half of the recommended amount and add a bit more liquid to absorb the powder until you get the consistency that works for you.

BEHOLD, THE BLENDERS

Like chef's knives or high-quality pots and pans, the blender you use to make your smoothies can have an enormous impact on the process. Some blenders blend dates and greens without a hitch, while others make chopped salad instead of a green smoothie. There are hundreds of blenders to choose from varying in price from under $20 to upward of $700, and finding the best blender to make smoothies is not as easy as it seems.

Here are some tips that might help you find the right blender for the types of smoothies that you want to enjoy.

Prep time: Some blenders are powerful enough to cut and blend large pieces of fruit and vegetables, while other blenders will require you to do some prep work before adding ingredients. Low-powered blenders generally won't blend up dates, whole nuts, or large chunks of fresh fruit or vegetables.

Container size: The size of the container will dictate the size of your smoothie. At a minimum, a 40-ounce container should be large enough to fill with nutrient-dense ingredients to yield about 24 ounces of drink. Most personal blenders have small containers, in the neighborhood of 20 to 24 ounces, while high-speed blenders can hold up to 64 ounces or more.

Container material: Most blenders are made from high-impact plastic, which is durable and light. BPA (Bisphenol A) is used to make plastic more durable, but at high temperatures and under acid conditions, BPA can leach into food. Due to these concerns, the U.S. Food and Drug Administration has banned the use of BPA in many products. Most blenders have BPA-free containers, but you might want to confirm this before making your purchase.

Power: If you are going to make blending smoothies a regular habit, then choose a blender with at least 700 watts of power. This is the power that will blend small nuts so that the consistency will be completely smooth without leftover chunks. The differences between wattage and horsepower can cause confusion when comparing blenders. For example, a 2-HP motor may draw 800 watts during use. Practically speaking, wattage is another way to rate the power, and the higher the wattage, the more power.

Warranty: Check the warranty before purchasing your blender. Less expensive blenders usually have a limited one-year warranty, while top-of-the-line blenders offer seven full years of coverage. Buying a blender from a reputable company is always a good idea.

Clean up: If you are going to have to spend twice as long cleaning your blender as you do using it, you will soon grow tired of the effort.

Special features: Do you want a blender that has a smoothie to-go cup option, food processing capability, or the ability to make dough? Some blenders are like a full-service kitchen, so you could save money in the long run by buying a more expensive model that will take the place of several appliances.

Reviews: Always read lots of reviews. Customers have no problem speaking their minds about their good and bad experiences with products, so it is worth spending several hours wading through the various comments.

At the end of the day, what's really most important is to consume healthy smoothies on a regular basis, not having the most expensive blender. To help you in your decision-making process, the the table in Appendix B (page 166) lists some of the more popular brands and their features.

BY THE NUMBERS

Starting your day with one of the healthy smoothies in this book can make a big difference in the quality of your diet. A typical smoothie in this book has three servings of fruits and/or vegetables, healthy fats, fiber, phytochemicals, vitamins, minerals, and protein. When compared to a seemingly healthy fast-food breakfast or one with cold cereal, you will see that you will get much more nutritional bang for your buck: no cholesterol, far less sodium, far more dietary fiber, healthy fats, moderate carbohydrates, no refined sugars, and adequate protein. The following chart provides a handy comparison.

	Apple Ginger Zinger Smoothie (page 75)	McDonald's Bacon, Egg & Cheese Bagel	2 cups Honey Nut Cheerios ½ banana ½ cup skim milk 1 cup orange juice
TOTAL CALORIES	380	620	500
TOTAL FAT	8g	31g	4g
SATURATED FAT (BAD FAT)	2g	11g	0g
UNSATURATED FAT (GOOD FAT)	6g	20g	4g
CHOLESTEROL	0mg	275mg	2mg
SODIUM	38mg	1,480mg	573mg
CARBOHYDRATES	62g	57g	106g
DIETARY FIBER	15g	3g	7g
PROTEIN	11g	30g	12g
SERVINGS OF FRUITS AND VEGETABLES	3	0	1½

TASTINESS TO GO

Though smoothies are typically slurped down as soon as they're made, sometimes you need to take one to go. If you have a blender with to-go cups, then you're all set! But chances are you don't, and you have been contemplating whether or not you should reuse the paper coffee cup that held your morning cup of joe. It's probably not a good idea to use paper for a thick, icy cold smoothie, so what exactly makes a great smoothie to-go bottle? Look for a bottle that is easy to clean, BPA-free, waterproof, easy to use, versatile, and large enough. Nothing is worse than trying to drink your smoothie out of an insulated coffee mug with a nickel size opening or having your greens get stuck in the spout. Use the following list to learn about the different to-go cup options available.

Hot/cold bottles. Reusable hot and cold bottles are tough and rough and may fit the bill if carrying glass makes you a bit nervous. Copco makes durable Sierra Tumblers that are BPA-free, hold 24 ounces of liquid, and have a nonslip grip for easy handling. Blender Bottles come with a wire blenderball that you can gently swirl to keep your smoothie ingredients emulsified. Wide-mouthed insulated coffee mugs will also do the trick and come in a variety of sizes and styles.

Mason jars. Glass mason jars make perfect to-go cups for smoothies. Glass is the best nonreactive container for everyday use because it doesn't leech any harmful chemicals into your body. Mason jars come in several shapes and sizes including 8 ounce, 16 ounce, and 32 ounce; wide mouth; or canning. Mason also makes BPA-free plastic freezer jars in 8 ounce and 16 ounce sizes, which are perfect for storing blended smoothies and prepped ingredients in the freezer.

Reusable lids that fit mason jars. The standard lid for a mason jar is made of metal, however, EcoJarz offers an earth-friendly, stainless steel drink top with a hole for a straw. Not only do these BPA-free lids fit mason jars, they come in a variety of sizes so that you can literally turn any old pasta jar or salsa jar into a smoothie to-go cup.

21 and Over

No, this isn't permission to toss a shot of vodka into your Mango Coconut Smoothie (page 90). Generally, it takes 21-plus days to form a new habit, which is the length of time chosen for this plan. According to *The Power of Habit: Why We Do What We Do in Life and Business*, habits consist of the following simple, but powerful, three-step loop:

1. Cue
2. Routine
3. Reward

When we start a new routine or task, our brains work hard to process new information. Eventually with repetition, the behavior becomes automatic, and the mental activity required to complete the task decreases dramatically.

Want to improve your health? Choose a cue, such as exercising as soon as you wake up; maintain that routine; and reward yourself with a healthy smoothie after each workout. Think about the smoothie, how delicious it will taste, and how it will energize you. Allow yourself to anticipate the reward. Eventually, that healthy craving will make it easier to push through your workout every day.

Reusable straws (metal and glass). If you are taking your smoothie to go, then you need something to slurp it through. EcoJarz also sells glass and metal smoothie straws with a small permanent bend for reaching those hard to get last dregs of smoothie. Also, if you are going to use a reusable straw, then you need to be able to clean it. Luckily, EcoJarz sells a handy dandy straw cleaner for easy cleaning—food safety first! You may also want to bust out a skinny spoon to stir and scoop your thick and creamy smoothie. Skinny spoons are great for reaching all the way down to the bottom of the jar for the last drop.

THE BUILDING BLOCKS

Here's where we get into the nitty gritty of making smoothies and where you will learn tips and tricks for concocting the perfect drink. There's something about the alchemy of tossing a few fruits, greens, ice, nuts, and liquid into a blender and ending up with a perfectly creamy and delicious smoothie that causes problems for many would-be smoothie enthusiasts. You may be holding back from drinking smoothies on a consistent basis because you haven't quite been able to capture the magic and your smoothies are either too green, too icy, or, well, something just isn't quite right. It really can be quite overwhelming with the number of possible ingredients and variables to tweak to get things just right. The good news is that anyone can learn how to make delicious smoothies. Once you get the basics down, you'll be blending up smoothie creations with all of your favorite ingredients.

HOW TO BUILD A SMOOTHIE

The process of building a smoothie is simple but important. The first step will be to choose the recipe you want to make, and this can be based on your purpose: Are you trying to get more greens into your diet? Do you need a healthy post-workout meal replacement? Are you trying to lose weight? Or do you just want a tasty snack? After you have chosen your recipe and gathered and prepped your ingredients, you will want to follow a basic step-by-step process for assembling and blending.

ADDING THE LIQUID

The first thing you will want to add to your blender is the liquid. Adding the liquid first helps float the ingredients; otherwise, they might get stuck on the blades and prevent your blender from processing. One to two cups of liquid should do the trick.

Another technique is to use the blender's blades to determine how much liquid base to add. Simply pour your liquid up to the tip of the blades until they are covered. If you like your smoothie to be thick, use less liquid, or if you prefer a consistency that will let you slurp your smoothie from a straw, use a bit more liquid. There are a number of different types of liquids you can use depending on your dietary taste and preferences, each lending a different characteristic. Individual liquids will be covered in the following section, Liquid Courage (see page 36).

ADDING THE BASE

The next thing you will want to add to the blender is your base. The base is what will give your smoothie its texture or body, adding both bulk and flavor. Creamy fruits like frozen bananas, mangos, and peaches all make great bases and add a nice sweet taste. Other great options are avocados, tofu, yogurt, and oatmeal.

ADDING THE INGREDIENTS

Adding fruits, vegetables, and other extras is the next step in building your smoothie. If you are adding frozen fruits and vegetables, you may need more liquid, as they will make the smoothie thicker. Likewise, the more fresh fruits and vegetables you include, the less liquid you will need. At this stage in the game, you may also want to add flavorings, sweeteners, nut butters, or seeds. This is where you take your smoothie nutrition to the next level.

BLENDER MAGIC

Once all of your ingredients are added, it's time to let your blender work its magic! Depending on the power of your blender and your smoothie ingredients, you may need to start out on a low setting before going up to top speed. Blend until the liquid is fully circulating within the blender for at least 5 to 10 seconds. It may take up to 60 seconds for the ingredients to be fully blended into a thick, creamy smoothie. Once blended, pour into a glass and enjoy!

Best Grab-'n'-Go Options

What to do when you are super slammed and need a smoothie quick? If you are following a vegan diet, beware that many bottled smoothies use whey-protein concentrate in their protein drinks, so always read the ingredient list. If your grab-'n'-go drink is going to replace a meal, pick one that has 10 or more grams of protein; otherwise, you may end up in a sugar coma.

For the best picks, turn to these trusty bottled brands and smoothie shacks:

- **Evolution Fresh:** Organic Avocado Greens, Super Green, Organic Splendid Carrot.

- **Jamba Juice:** Choose from the Whole Food Nutrition Smoothies, the Fit 'N Fruitful Smoothies, or the Functional Smoothies. All smoothies are made to order.

- **Juice Generation Smoothie Stores:** Peanut Butter Split, Protein Buzz, Joyful Almond.

- **Naked Juice:** Protein Zone: Made from 100 percent juice, vegan, with added soy protein.

- **Odwalla Mango Protein:** Made from 100 percent juice, vegan, with added soy protein.

- **Odwalla Original Super Protein:** Made from 100 percent juice, vegan, with added soy protein.

- **Vega Protein Smoothie:** If you have a BlenderBottle container, you can whip up a smoothie in a few seconds by using this nutrient-rich powder. Just add a serving of the powder to the container, add water or nondairy milk, and swirl the wire blender ball around until the powder dissolves.

LIQUID COURAGE

Using coconut water, juice, tea, or coffee will make a big difference in the end results of your smoothies. Liquids vary in texture, taste, and nutrition, and becoming familiar with some of the main characteristics of each will help you become a pro at putting together your own recipes. Liquids can add body, flavor, fiber, protein, and other nutrients like caffeine and antioxidants. Liquids can also add a lot of additional calories, fat, and sugar, which could push your smoothie into the not-so-healthy category. Keeping portions in check and reading nutrition labels will be important if weight loss is your goal. Watery fruits like watermelon, pineapple, and oranges can also take the place of some of the liquid in your smoothies—the possibilities are limitless. Use the following list to get to know your liquid options.

Almond milk: Almond milks come in a number of varieties and can range from 30 to 120 calories per cup, with or without added sugars. Almond milk is lactose- and cholesterol-free and a great source of calcium, vitamins A and D, and B vitamins. However, don't count on it for protein as it contains a negligible amount.

MYOM: Make Your Own Milk

Making your own nut milk at home is amazingly simple! It is just a matter of soak, blend, strain, and store. This recipe calls for almonds, but any nut will work.

1 cup raw almonds

Water for soaking nuts

3 cups water

2 Medjool dates, pitted (for sweetness)

½ teaspoon vanilla extract

Pinch salt

MAKES APPROXIMATELY 4 CUPS OF MILK

1. Soak the almonds in water overnight or for at least six hours. Drain the water from the almonds and discard.

2. Blend the 3 cups of water, almonds, dates, vanilla extract, and salt until well blended and almost smooth. Strain the blended almond mixture using a cheesecloth or other strainer by placing the cloth over a large bowl and pouring the nut mixture into the bowl to strain the liquid. Pull the cheesecloth up, twist it, and wring until all of the excess moisture is out.

3. Transfer the liquid to a glass bottle and store in the fridge. Homemade raw almond milk will keep well in the refrigerator for three to four days.

The amount of body almond milk adds to your smoothie will depend on the calorie count: The lower-calorie versions have little to no fat or carbohydrates, while the higher-calorie versions have carbohydrate calories coming from sugar as well as a few grams of fat. Even the lowest-calorie milks can give a smoothie an added flavor dimension, extra thickness, and a hint of sweetness, in addition to a nutrition boost.

Coconut milk: Coconut milk found in the refrigerated section is entirely different from the coconut milk you will find in a can. Cold coconut milk shares a number of characteristics with the other nondairy milks: It is lactose- and cholesterol-free; fortified with calcium, vitamins A and D, and B vitamins; and comes sweetened or unsweetened in a range of calorie levels. Unsweetened coconut milk has a neutral taste and can add body to a smoothie without being overpowering. Canned coconut milk is squeezed from the meat of the coconut, which produces a sweet and tasty liquid. Though it is high in fiber, it is also high in calories and fat, so as a liquid base you may want to reserve it for those special dessert-like smoothie indulgences.

Coconut water: Coconut water is low in calories, fat, and sugar, and is filled with electrolytes like potassium, making it a great liquid base for before or after a work-out. Coconut water won't add to the consistency of a smoothie, but it will add a touch of sweetness and a dose of hydrating nutrients.

Cold coffee: Skip the high-calorie, high-fat coffee drink at your local cafe and use cold coffee to create your own healthy iced Frappuccino. Coffee beans differ in their acidity, aroma, and body, and flavors range from earthy to bitter to buttery tasting, so the choice of bean will be a matter of personal preference. The most convenient way to use coffee as your liquid is simply to brew it and store it in the refrigerator until it cools. It is best to use it within a day; otherwise, the longer it sits the more bitter it will get. Coffee will add a depth and body to your smoothie along with a dose of antioxidants and phytochemicals. Caffeinated or decaffein-ated, coffee pairs well with a dash of cacao and sweet fruits like strawberries and cherries. Another tip is to use up the last drop of your morning brew by pouring the leftovers into ice cube trays.

Hemp milk: Hemp milk is one of the newer milks on the scene. It is a modestly creamy beverage with a slightly nutty, malt-like flavor. Nutritionally, a typical brand of unsweetened hemp milk has about 80 calories per cup; is fortified with calcium, vitamins A and D, and B vitamins; and contains about two grams of protein per serving. Hemp milk does have more fat than the other nondairy milks, with about eight grams of unsaturated fat per serving. The fat in the milk is what makes hemp richer than rice, almond, and coconut milk, so it will add a bit more creaminess to your smoothie. Hemp milk can be an acquired taste, so taste it plain before you add it to your smoothie.

Juices (apple, orange, cranberry): Fresh squeezed juices contain an array of vitamins, minerals, and antioxidants, and can give a smoothie a refreshing flavor boost. Fruit juices are high in natural sugars, so be certain to combine them with low-glycemic fruits like peaches, berries, and apples; with greens; or with ingredients that contain protein like tofu or nuts and seeds. For a flavor and nutrient boost with less sugar, use ½ cup of juice mixed with ½ cup of water. Stick to juices that are 100-percent juice without added sugars.

Tasty Terms

Antioxidants: In the body, substances that significantly decrease adverse effects of free radicals on normal physiological function.

Aseptically: A system of packaging sterilized products in airtight containers so that freshness is preserved for several months.

Healthy fats: Healthy fats include monounsaturated fats and polyunsaturated fats. Omega-3 fats are a type of polyunsaturated fat. Healthy fats tend to decrease total cholesterol and bad cholesterol; they also contribute to heart health. Omega-3 fats decrease the inflammation associated with heart disease.

Isoflavone: A phytoestrogen produced chiefly by plants of the legume family, especially soybeans. Isoflavones are potentially useful in lowering cholesterol and in treating some cancers and menopausal symptoms.

Minerals: Inorganic elements. Some minerals are essential nutrients that the body requires in small amounts.

Phytochemicals: Nonnutrient compounds found in plants that act as antioxidants and are considered to be beneficial to human health.

Polyphenols: An alcohol group that occurs naturally in plants, and some kinds, such as flavonoids and tannins, are believed to be beneficial to health.

Probiotics: A dairy food or a dietary supplement containing live bacteria that replaces or adds to the beneficial bacteria normally present in the gastrointestinal tract.

Triglycerides: A naturally occurring fat found in animal tissues and some vegetables; an important energy source forming much of the fat stored in the body.

Vitamins: Any of a group of organic substances essential in small quantities in the body for normal metabolism. Vitamins are found in minute amounts in natural foodstuffs or produced synthetically.

Milk: Dairy milk is a common choice. All types work well in smoothies because they have a smooth and neutral taste, allowing your other ingredients to take center stage. Anything but skim will have dietary cholesterol, and as fat content rises, so will the amount per cup. A perk with dairy milk is that it will boost the protein content of your smoothie. An eight-ounce glass of milk contains eight grams of high-quality protein, along with calcium, vitamins A and D, and B vitamins.

Rice milk: Rice milk is, honestly, kind of thin and runny. With that said, if allergies or lactose intolerance are a concern, rice milk can be a good choice. There are a number of varieties to choose from: flavored, unflavored, and high- and low-calorie. Most rice milks are fortified with calcium, vitamins A and D, and B vitamins, but like coconut and almond milks, it will have little to no protein. If you simply want to add calcium, vitamin D, and other nutrients to your smoothie, and you don't like the taste of almond or soy milk, then rice milk is a good choice. However, it won't add much in terms of body and creaminess.

Soy milk: Soy milk is a great source of protein, calcium, vitamins A and D, B vitamins, and isoflavones. It doesn't have lactose or cholesterol, but it does have a distinctive taste—sort of like pureed tofu. Using soy milk in your smoothie will make it creamy and rich, but it will also influence the taste. If this is a concern, pair it with stronger flavored fruits like raspberries and blueberries. The calorie count of soy milk is generally in the 90- to 120-calorie range per cup. It doesn't get much lower than this due to the presence of protein and a gram or two of fat, but the added protein can help you stay full longer and make your smoothie more satisfying.

Tea: Using brewed and cooled teas as your liquid base can expand your flavor options as well as your intake of phytochemicals and antioxidants. Green tea makes a great base for a green smoothie: It is rich in a type of polyphenol that acts as an antioxidant, decreasing the development of chronic disease, but it does have caffeine. Other teas that add a flavor boost are chamomile, blueberry rooibos, and peppermint. While tea won't add much in terms of body or creaminess, it makes up for this by supplying your body with phytonutrients. Brew and chill your tea before adding it to your smoothie.

Water: Water is essential for your body, and when you are properly hydrated, you have more energy. Water is inexpensive, easy, and allows you to get your calories from highly nutritious fruits, vegetables, and other select ingredients.

Ice, Ice, Maybe?

Though many people assume that ice is a key ingredient to smoothies, it's really more of a filler. Depending on the recipe, frozen fruit or vegetables do just as good of a job thickening and cooling your beverage without diluting the other flavors. Frozen ingredients also act as an emulsifier in your smoothie to give it texture and body and to keep the liquids and solids from separating too quickly. Start by using just a few ice cubes in your smoothies until you find the texture and consistency that works for you. To avoid diluting your smoothie, freeze almond milk in ice cube trays. If you have more fresh fruit than frozen fruit, you will want to use about six ice cubes to give the smoothie a thicker texture. Mixing in extra ice can also tone down the sweetness if you run into a smoothie snafu.

TURN UP THE BASE

The next step to building your smoothie is choosing a base, or filler. Bases are what make smoothies thick, creamy, and filling, especially if you are not using a creamy fruit like mangos or bananas. For example, a smoothie that uses apples, a non-creamy fruit, will need something like oats, pumpkin, or frozen fruit to achieve a thick, nongrainy texture. Many recipes combine several different bases to round out the nutrition profile, achieve the right texture, and blend flavors. Frozen bananas are a popular choice because they have a neutral taste that goes well with just about anything, and they make smoothies thick and creamy. Don't be afraid to think outside the box with bases. Cooked grains like quinoa and buckwheat go great in smoothies. You can't go wrong with canned or fresh pumpkin, cooked butternut squash, or cooked sweet potato with or without the skin. Do some experimentation with your favorite foods, and you will soon realize which ones contribute to the taste and texture of your smoothie in ways that you like.

Here are a few common base options to try.

Avocado: An avocado may not seem like a go-to smoothie ingredient, but if you're skeptical, don't be. Avocados provide a uniquely silky texture to smoothies, and when blended with ingredients that are sweet, they add body and richness. Avocados are like a magic ingredient that will completely transform your smoothie game. This decadent-tasting fruit is rich in potassium, dietary fiber, and mono-unsaturated fats and will instantly boost the nutrient density of your smoothie. Avocados work great fresh, or you can freeze them in ¼- and ½-cup portions for added thickness anytime. After putting avocado in your smoothie, you may never make a smoothie without it again—just watch the portion sizes: Half of one medium avocado is about 130 calories.

Fresh fruit: When using fresh fruit as your base, there are some key principles to keep in mind which will prevent you from ending up with a runny smoothie or a glass of pulpy fruit juice. Creamy fruits like mango, banana, peach, pear, and papaya all work well in fresh form. If fresh fruits will be your primary base, try adding ¼ cup avocado or oats for some extra creaminess. Water-rich fruits like watermelon, oranges, and pineapple won't give you that creamy consistency, but they can be used successfully—just adjust by adding a thickener like ice, avocado, or oats, and cut down on the amount of liquid you use.

Frozen fruit: Frozen fruits make a great smoothie base and can serve double duty by taking the place of ice. Peaches, strawberries, blueberries, raspberries, bananas, mangos, and cherries are all popular choices. Bananas are great for added thick-ness, but they have a fairly neutral taste, so toss in some strawberries or peaches for added sweetness. Some good flavor combinations include banana as the base with strawberries, apple as the base with blueberries, and mango as the base with pineapple.

Oats/oatmeal: Using oats gives vegan smoothies a nutritional boost and adds thickness and body. There are two options when adding oats to your smoothie: raw or cooked. The quickest and most convenient option is to just dump the oats in along with everything else. The other is to grind them in a spice grinder or add them to your blender first. Then process them for a few seconds before adding the rest of the ingredients. The former will give your smoothie some added texture, so experiment to find out what you prefer. You can also use cooked oats or other types of cooked grains. It's best to precook them and allow them to cool com-pletely before use.

Tofu: Adding tofu to smoothies is a great way to give your drink extra staying power so that it keeps you feeling full and energized. Tofu is high in protein, and it creates a smooth, silky texture when added to drinks. Tofu comes in a number of varieties: silken, firm, extra firm, water-packed, and aseptically packaged. Silken tofu is the softest type and blends the easiest, but any type of tofu will work in

GREEN MACHINES

FOOD: 1 CUP SERVING	CALORIES	PROTEIN (GRAMS)	FIBER (GRAMS)	STANDOUT NUTRIENTS
ARUGULA	6	0.6	0.4	Vitamin A
BOK CHOY	9	1.0	0.7	Vitamin A
BROCCOLI	31	2.6	2.4	Vitamin C
CELERY	16	0.7	1.6	Vitamin A & C
CUCUMBER (WITH PEEL)	16	0.7	0.5	Vitamin C
KALE (LOOSELY PACKED)	8	0.7	0.6	Vitamin A & C
LETTUCE (BIBB)	7	1.0	1.0	Vitamin A
LETTUCE (ICEBERG)	10	1.0	1.0	Vitamin A
LETTUCE (ROMAINE)	8	0.6	1.0	Vitamin A
SPINACH	7	0.9	0.7	Vitamin A

smoothies. If you choose silken, you may have to use less liquid and vice versa if you toss in tofu that is extra firm. Tofu can also be frozen in ice cube trays, making it great to keep on hand for added thickness and protein anytime.

Yogurt: The number of yogurt options available is mind-boggling. Yogurt can turn a lack-luster smoothie into one that is rich, creamy, and satisfying. If you are following a vegan diet, you can choose from soy, coconut, almond, and rice varieties. Soy will have the most distinctive taste and will also be the one to choose if you are looking for a protein boost. Coconut, almond, and rice will have very little, if any, protein, so make your choice based on your nutritional needs. Each type will vary in the number of calories as well as the amount of added sugars. Stick to plain, unsweetened, or vanilla flavor, as they tend to have the least amount of additional ingredients.

SPECIAL EXTRAS

Add-ins, or special extras, enhance both the flavor and nutrition of smoothies. Add-ins can contribute thickness and give your smoothie some extra jazz and a dose of character. Add-ins may simply be an additional serving of fruit or vegetables to go with your base. For example, adding a serving of kale or spinach to a smoothie with frozen fruit as the base can instantly transform it into a green smoothie.

An abundance of "superfoods," like maca, lucuma, spirulina, wheat grass, bee pollen, acai powder, aloe, and green food powders, are available to boost the power of your smoothies. Peruse the superfood section of your local health-food store and you will find a dizzying array of options, each with a distinctive taste and nutrition profile. As your smoothie-making skills and tastes develop, you will instinctively know which to add to which recipes. Of course, not every smoothie will include each add-in, so the list below is meant to give you an idea of what's possible.

Frozen fruit: Frozen fruits make an excellent base to any smoothie, but they can also be used as an extra special add-in to boost the nutrition superpowers of your smoothie further. Cherries and blueberries are rich in antioxidants and phyto-chemicals, and adding a serving or two per day to your diet can help decrease your risk for a number of chronic diseases.

Frozen greens: You can turn any smoothie into a green smoothie by adding a cup or two of frozen greens. Kale and spinach are mild in taste, and by mixing them with a sweet fruit like berries, you won't even know they are there. Frozen greens will add thickness to your smoothies, making them more filling. High in vitamins A and C, adding a serving or two is a great way to increase the amount of greens in your diet and your kids' diet too.

Frozen vegetables: Frozen edamame in a smoothie? You betcha! Edamame can take your ho-hum green smoothie nutrition to the next level. High in protein, fiber, and phytochemicals, adding ½ cup of shelled edamame to a smoothie will add a whopping 10 grams of complete high-quality protein, 6 grams of fiber, and only 120 calories. Frozen green peas are also a great source of protein, and they are naturally sweet and high in fiber. Peas give smoothies a creamy, sweet taste and will keep you feeling full longer. Try using a ¼ cup of peas combined with almond milk, frozen spinach, mango, tofu, avocado, and a dash of lime, mint, or ginger. You can add any frozen vegetable to a smoothie—just adjust the liquid based on the water content of the vegetable you are adding.

Powder Power?

Unless you live at the gym, it's unlikely that you'll need to bulk up your smoothie (or your body!) with added protein powders. The recipes in this book are protein powder-free, but if you are inclined to add a little boost, try a chocolate- or vanilla-flavored variety, as they are usually the tastiest. Of course, listen to that commonsense voice in your head that tells you that a chocolate protein powder might not be the most delicious addition to a peach-ginger smoothie.

Vegan protein powders are generally made from rice, pea, hemp, artichoke heart, sacha inchi, or other sprouted grains. Some powders are just protein isolates or concentrates, while others are meal replacements with added fiber, fruit and vegetable extracts, vitamins, minerals, and even probiotics. Each type of powder has a distinctive texture and taste, and some are pretty grainy, while others are quite smooth. Start with half of the recommended serving and play around until you have a texture and taste you like.

Nuts and nut butters: Nuts and nut butters add healthy fats, fiber, protein, magnesium, and vitamin E to smoothies. Some nuts, like hazelnuts, are also rich in copper and zinc, while almonds have calcium and folate, and peanuts are a good source of niacin. All nuts contain antioxidants and phytochemicals, and including one ounce per day can reduce the risk for developing chronic diseases. Nuts and nut butters will make a smoothie rich and thick, but they are calorie-dense, so keep an eye on portion sizes.

Powders: There are a plethora of powders you can add to your smoothie to boost the nutrition content. If you are making an after-workout smoothie or simply want to get more protein into your diet, add in a high-quality protein powder. Powders can also nutritionally balance smoothies that don't include another source of protein like tofu, nuts, or beans.

Wheat and barley grass powders are high in chlorophyll, an alkalizing nutrient, as well as a number of vitamins and minerals. The grasses claim to have a number of health benefits, including improving eczema and digestion. Spirulina is another green powder high in chlorophyll, and on a per calorie basis, it is also a good source of protein and B vitamins. Keep in mind that any of the green powders will turn your smoothie green! They may also give your smoothie a bit of a grass-like taste, so pair them with strongly flavored fruits like berries.

Another powder definitely worth trying is cacao. Raw cacao is minimally processed and contains flavonoids, a type of antioxidant that can lower bad cholesterol and blood pressure. Raw cacao is bitter, so it will need to be combined with some natural sweeteners. Maca is a root that you can buy in powdered form, and it is thought to increase virility and improve energy and mood. It has a very distinctive, chalky taste, so start with a small quantity until you find your preferred taste.

Seeds: Seeds are nutritional powerhouses and can be added to smoothies without changing the taste. Chia seeds are low in calories, with 60 calories per two tablespoons. Each serving has three grams of heart-healthy omega-3 fats, five grams of fiber, and three grams of protein. Chia seeds make an excellent thickener. Add one or two tablespoons to a small amount of water and allow the seeds to sit for about 10 minutes until they form a gel.

Hemp seeds are another superfood. One-ounce has 170 calories. 14 grams of heart-healthy fats, 3 grams of which are omega-3 fats; and 10 grams of plant-based protein. Hemp seeds also make great thickeners. Add the seeds to your liquid first and process into a paste before adding the rest of the ingredients.

Pumpkin, sesame, and sunflower are all equally nutritious seeds, with each containing a distinctive array of nutrients.

Cool Cubes

An ice cube tray is great for freezing herbs and other ingredients to use for a flavor boost in your smoothies. Consider buying silicone ice cube trays; they make it easier to remove the frozen cubes. Once frozen, you can transfer the cubes to a zip-top bag for storage in the freezer.

To freeze fresh greens like spinach and kale, cook them first, then puree in a food processor or blender, and then pour into the trays and freeze. To freeze fresh herbs (like basil, parsley, and mint), just rinse, chop, pack the trays about two-thirds full of herbs, and cover with water, milk, or juice. You can use one herb per cube or mix two or three together in one cube. Herbs tend to float to the top and may get freezer burned, so cover lightly with plastic wrap before freezing. Remember to label each tray or bag of cubes with the type of herb.

Coffee, juice, yogurt, bananas, and almond milk are some other ingredients that you can freeze to add a dash of extra flavor to your smoothies any time.

Spices and flavorings: You can give your smoothie a dessert-like taste by adding dried spices like cinnamon, nutmeg, ginger, and allspice, just as you would in a baked recipe but in smaller quantities. Extracts such as peppermint, almond, lemon, and vanilla can enhance the flavor of your smoothie and make it insanely delicious. Because they are concentrated, you will only need about ⅛ to ¼ a teaspoon.

Fresh herbs can be used to give your smoothie a more savory spin: Basil, parsley, dill, chives, cilantro, and mint are all great choices. Just chop finely before adding and start with 1 or 2 tablespoons until you find your desired taste. Adding molasses to a smoothie will pump up the iron content, a mineral that is often lacking in a vegan diet. Try adding ½ tablespoon for a hint of sweetness without being overpowering.

Sweeteners: If you are worried that your smoothie won't taste sweet enough, you can give it a little help. Medjool dates are by far the crème de la crème of smoothie sweeteners. With a caramel-like taste, dates are compatible with most flavors, adding both sweetness and nutrition. For a no-calorie, natural sweetener, try adding liquid or powdered Stevia. Some brands have added ingredients for easy mixing, so read the nutrition labels and taste before adding to your smoothie. Maple syrup, agave, and brown rice syrup will add distinctive flavors as well as additional calories in the form of sugar, so keep an eye on portion sizes. Really ripe frozen bananas are another great method for sweetening smoothies that you may want to try.

CHAPTER 3

HOW TO USE THE PLAN

Here is where we get into the nuts and bolts of how to use the plan in this book. Every day thousands of people make the decision to start eating better and to lose weight; yet every day those thousands of people don't really have a plan or any idea of what they are doing. After all, there are so many decisions to be made: Should I eat carbs? Should I eliminate fat? Which fruits and vegetables should I be eating? Should I count calories?

"Do the best you can, with what you have, where you are."
—Teddy Roosevelt

The plan in this book is meant to help you on your journey to better health and weight management by educating you on how to implement small, permanent dietary changes that you can live with until they become a habit. Eating healthier is not about deprivation or never eating your favorite foods. Rather, healthy eating focuses on nourishing your body with whole, unprocessed foods, and balancing your intake with physical activity so that you can move toward living a better life.

Before undertaking any type of change, there is a bit of mental preparation involved, along with becoming familiar with some key principles that can ensure your success. The following section includes tips to get you off to a good start.

TIPS FOR SUCCESS

Make a firm commitment. Before you begin the plan, get clear on why you are doing it. Take some time to identify two or three reasons you want to improve your diet. The reasons should be visceral and so powerful so that in moments when you want to give up, you can turn to these reasons for strength to carry on. Write your reasons for change on Post-it notes and put them where you can see them every day.

Set realistic goals. Losing weight and improving health is a long-term goal, so it is important to be realistic about what you are hoping to achieve by the end of the plan. Know that there will be days when things just go wrong. But stick to it. You can do this! Better eating habits and physical activity will help you live longer and feel better, and you will set a good example for those around you.

Reserve time to thoroughly review the 3-day cleanse and 21-day meal plan. The following sections explain the plan in depth; however, plan on taking some time to read through everything several times before you begin. The plan is all about what and how much you eat, with an emphasis on quality, balance, and portion control.

Do a pantry and kitchen clean-out. Before you start the plan in this book, you should set aside time to do a pantry and kitchen clean-out. If your house is full of unhealthy foods, it will be difficult for you to focus on building new healthy habits. Don't worry; once it is clean, you can load it back up with fresh, unprocessed foods.

A kitchen clean-out can be done in a number of quick and easy steps: Inspect ingredient labels and remove any foods that contain trans fats, hydrogenated oils, sugar as the first or second ingredient, and artificial sweeteners; check expiration dates and get rid of expired foods; get rid of highly processed snacks foods like cookies and candy. If you're getting rid of unopened, unexpired goods, donate them to a local charity, food bank, or shelter. Make room on your kitchen counter for a bowl of fresh fruit.

Plan when you go shopping and do food prep. The plan will include weekly shopping lists and suggested pantry items; however, before you begin, choose a shopping day or two and mark it on your calendar. As soon as you get home from your shopping trips, follow through: Wash and store your fruits and vegetables, and review and complete the weekly prep instructions. Stack up glass containers of prepped ingredients in the refrigerator and freezer, and bask in your own awesome preparedness.

Be strategic about freezing. The freezer is your friend. Prep and freeze cubes of nondairy milks, coffee, tea, herbs, fruits, veggies, and tofu. Whirl up a batch of smoothies and store them in eight-ounce stackable freezer jars.

Focus on adding healthy foods. Many people focus on what they "can't" or "shouldn't" eat when eating healthy. Practice focusing on what you can and should eat. Instead of focusing on eating less junk food, focus on eating more good stuff. Get excited about all of the fresh, tasty, whole foods you'll be consuming each day: meals that satisfy you and truly nourish your body and soul.

Enlist support. Whether you are doing the plan with a friend, partner, coworker, or going it alone, it will be important to enlist support from people who share similar goals. Think in terms of assembling a "pit crew" of like-minded people who can be a source of inspiration and encouragement, especially when the going gets tough.

Create your habit cues. Remember that habits consist of a simple, but powerful, three-step loop: First there is a cue, then there is the routine, and finally there is the reward. Decide what your cue will be for including your daily healthy smoothie and salad.

Practice self-awareness. You know yourself best. Tune into your hunger levels and the way your emotions affect your eating decisions. You know your daily eating habits and which situations generally derail your efforts. Use the plan in this book to stay on track and focus on your strengths as you improve your self-confidence.

Focus on what is within your control. As you go through the plan, focus on your behaviors, not the outcomes. Set aside what you can't control and focus on what you can do, right now, today. Do your shopping, set aside time to prep your recipes, and focus on eating healthy and being active.

Get moving! Eating healthfully is only part of the formula for successful weight loss and improvements in health. Getting regular physical activity is the other portion. Exercise is a powerful tool, helping you burn calories, reduce stress, increase strength, and improve your overall health. Along with making a daily healthy smoothie a habit, set some specific goals for being active.

Get enough sleep. A single night of less sleep can dial down your metabolism and set off stress hormones that can trigger an increase in appetite. Try going to bed earlier so you wake up feeling refreshed and so that you have time to be active and make a healthy smoothie.

Celebrate little victories. Big or small, celebrating every victory is important when making any type of change, and this is especially true at the start of a new meal plan. You had a smoothie with spinach for the first time and liked it—celebrate! Call a friend or get a hug from a spouse. It's the little victories that add up to success in the long run.

Drink enough water. People often confuse thirst with hunger, so be certain you are hydrating yourself throughout the day. When you are using the plan and eating the suggested smoothies and salads each day, you will be meeting part of your fluid requirements. Include water with each meal or another no-calorie drink, and you will be keeping your metabolism revved and your body processes humming along.

If weight loss is your goal, know your numbers. The plan begins with a 3-day detox, which includes three healthy smoothies per day, totaling approximately 1,200 calories per day. For women, this is the minimum safe amount of calories recommended for weight loss without significantly lowering metabolic rate. For men, this number is 1,800 calories per day, which is why there is a list of suggested supplemental snacks included in the plan. If weight loss is your goal, you may find it useful to determine your daily calorie requirements before starting the plan.

Join the clean slate club. There will be days when things don't go right. You get up late, you forgot to bring your salad to work, and you got caught in traffic so you missed your spin class. Lose the all-or-none thinking, clean the slate, and get back on track. Life happens, and there will never be a perfect time to start a healthy-eating plan. The only time is now.

THE 3-DAY DETOX CLEANSE

The plan in this book begins with a 3-day detox cleanse, which includes three smoothies per day. This cleanse should not be confused with a fast; you will be drinking three nutritionally dense, filling, and delicious smoothies each day, along with balanced supplemental snacks, depending on your individual calorie needs and health and weight-loss goals.

Everything you need to know to be successful with your 3-day detox cleanse will be explained in advance. Suggestions for when you might start your plan, along with strategies for carving out some relaxed downtime to complete your plan, will be discussed. A complete shopping list will be included for the full three days of smoothies so that you can take the list to the grocery store and buy everything that you need for the cleanse before you begin.

Before you make your first smoothie, read through the entire recipe once, make sure you have all of your prepped ingredients at the ready, then toss them into your blender, give them a whirl, and get ready for a delicious, filling, and nutritious smoothie. Every blender is different, so don't be afraid to add more liquid if your smoothie is too thick, cut back on ice, skip the ice in favor of frozen fruit, or follow one of the suggested variations or substitutions included with each recipe.

Be prepared for a bit of experimentation as you become familiar with the characteristics of different ingredients and the workings of your individual blender. Refer back to the Troubleshooting Guide in Chapter 1 (see page 24) for additional tips and solutions to common smoothie problems. It won't take long before you become a super smoothie chef!

FOOD PREPARATION

The plan includes a detailed list of the food preparation tasks that you need to do in advance for each of the three days. Doing the shopping and the advance food prep will be a key to your success and will ensure that you have everything you need to get started before you begin the plan.

THE DAYS

In addition to three smoothie recipes, each day of the 3-day detox cleanse includes the following elements:

- **Tip:** These items add to your healthy eating education so that you will be simultaneously increasing your nutrition know-how while improving your diet. You know what they say: Knowledge is power.

- **Intention:** The purpose of intentions is to aim the mind in a desired direction. Most of the time our minds are caught up in thoughts, emotions, and a noisy internal dialogue. Much of that inner dialogue is negative and can sabotage our efforts. Read the intention each day. Use it as an anchor to redirect your thoughts and quiet your mind so that you can stay focused on your goals.
- **Encouragement:** This is an inspirational quote to keep you feeling empowered and to fuel your self-confidence for making positive changes in your life.
- **Nutritional info:** Each of the recipes serves one and includes the nutrient breakdown with information listed for total calories, total fat, total carbohydrates, dietary fiber, and protein.

Use this information to keep you on track, inspire, and motivate you. You may find it helpful to pick out quotes or intentions that you find particularly useful and write them on Post-it notes and put them where you can see them—for example, on the refrigerator, bathroom mirror, and your computer.

CALORIES AND CARBOHYDRATES

Before you start the cleanse, you may find it helpful to have a little nutrition know-how and an understanding that not all calories are created equal: 1,200 calories from Twinkies is not the same as 1,200 calories from nutrient-dense smoothies. Each smoothie consists of high-quality plant proteins, antioxidant-rich fruits and vegetables, slow-burning carbohydrates, and heart-healthy fats. The protein sources in the smoothies are all plant based, and the combinations within the smoothies ensures that your body will be getting all of the essential amino acids it needs. The plant sources of protein include soymilk, tofu, protein-fortified almond milk, nuts, seeds, and beans. Protein is included with every meal and in every snack because protein is the most satiating nutrient, meaning protein is what will keep you full.

The carbohydrate sources are all high quality and unrefined, consisting of a mix of simple and complex carbohydrates. Simple carbohydrates are found in antioxidant-rich fresh fruits, and complex carbohydrates are found in fiber-rich vegetables, beans, legumes, and whole grains. Carbohydrates are a necessary part of any balanced diet: They provide fuel for your working muscles, feed your brain, and keep your blood sugar even.

FAT CONTENT AND SNACKS

Each smoothie includes heart-healthy fats. Don't be afraid of the fat content: Fat is absolutely critical to your body and should be included in any healthy diet plan.

The majority of fats in your diet should be healthy monounsaturated fats—such as almonds, avocados, hemp seeds, cashews, and nut butters.

Feelings of deprivation or hunger shouldn't be an issue if you eat the three recommended smoothies each day while you are doing the 3-day detox cleanse. However, depending on your individual needs and level of physical activity, the calorie level may be lower than you are used to, so feel free to choose from the list of recommended snacks to supplement your diet.

THE 21-DAY PLAN

After you have successfully completed your 3-day detox cleanse, you'll be ready for the 21-day plan of healthy smoothies and salads. Or, skip the 3-day detox and ease into the world of smoothies by starting off with the 21-day plan. The 21-day plan will be broken down into three separate 7-day meal plans. Each week will contain the same following elements:

- Menu at a Glance
- Pantry Items & Shopping List
- Prep
- Smoothies Shopping List
- Suggested Salads Shopping List
- Weekly Wrap-Up

Take time on the weekend to do your shopping and advance food preparation, stocking your fridge, freezer, and pantry with healthy ingredients. Then when Monday morning rolls around, all you have to do is just grab 'n' go. Healthy eating doesn't have to be complicated!

Each day of the plan will include a suggested salad recipe for you to use as one of your other meals. Enjoying a healthy salad as one of your other meals will simplify your food decisions even further. At the same time, you'll increase the nutrient density of your diet and get closer to improving your health. Forget what you thought about salads being for rabbits. The salads in this book are filling, good tasting, balanced, and nutritionally complete. Most importantly, they're super easy to throw together—no cooking required! Each salad is meant to be a meal and will meet the caloric needs of most moderately active females. If you are male, you may want to increase the portions or have one of the snacks listed in Chapter 4: The 3-Day Detox Cleanse (see page 66) along with your salad. Salad recipes are listed in Chapter 8 (see page 143).

Concentrate on the few simple habits, tasks, and actions that truly matter right now. Most of all, embrace all of the wonderful possibilities that await you and your health as you add nutrient-rich foods to your diet.

Keep this in mind as you move forward:

"The secret of health for both mind and body is not to mourn for the past, worry about the future, or anticipate troubles, but to live in the present moment wisely and earnestly." —Buddha

VARIATIONS, SUBSTITUTIONS, AND ADDITIONS

Each smoothie will have a short recipe descriptor highlighting the health benefits of the main ingredients and include two variations on the basic recipe so that they are more customizable to specific tastes and nutrition needs.

VARIATIONS AND SUBSTITUTIONS

One variation will be a substitution, and one variation will be an addition. For the substitution, it may be for the liquid, the base, or one of the special extras. Feel free to use the information in Chapter 2: The Building Blocks (see page 33) to make your own substitutions. When making substitutions, just keep in mind that you should switch out ingredients that have similar characteristics so that your smoothie doesn't end up with a snafu. For example, if you are switching out frozen fruit for fresh, remember to reduce the amount of liquid in your smoothie. If you are substituting soy milk for almond, be aware that it will be thicker and there may be an effect on the taste.

ADDITIONS

The additions include suggestions for modifying the flavor, changing the texture, or increasing the calorie count. For example, if you want to customize your smoothie and make it a post-workout recovery drink, add ¼ cup of oats for a complex carbohydrate boost to refuel your muscles. You may also want to use additions for supercharging the nutritional content by adding special extras like chia seeds or maca power. The most important thing to remember when making smoothies is to have fun and let your creativity shine!

LABELS

Labels will accompany many of the smoothies to indicate the following categories of smoothies and their nutritional benefits:

- **Beauty-boosting:** High in vitamins A, C, and E; biotin; zinc; omega-3 fats; and antioxidants.
- **Brain-boosting:** High in antioxidants, vitamin E, and monounsaturated fats.
- **Heart-healthy:** High in monounsaturated fats, omega-3 fats, B vitamins, and soluble fiber.
- **High-fiber:** More than 10 grams of fiber per serving.
- **Joint-supporting:** High in anti-inflammatory foods, antioxidants, omega-3 fats, and vitamins C, D, and E.
- **Low-calorie:** Less than 300 calories per serving.
- **Protein-packed:** More than 15 grams of protein per serving.

PART 2
THE PLAN

CHAPTER 4

THE 3-DAY DETOX CLEANSE

Now that you know how to make nutritious smoothies, get ready for your 3-day detox cleanse. If you typically start your day by hitting the snooze button a couple of times until you can manage to drag yourself out of bed, you may need something other than coffee.

The human body is designed to naturally remove toxins and cleanse itself. However, even under the best of circumstances, it has a tough job digesting saturated fat and protein and processing high volumes of additives, preservatives, salt, and sugar. By recognizing the signs that your body isn't working at its best, you can do something about it before you have out-of-control weight gain and the chronic diseases that can result from it.

On your 3-day detox cleanse, you can expect to nourish your body with clean food and drinks, while you allow your body's natural healing mechanism to take over. The focus will be on quality not quantity, and you can anticipate consuming about 1,200 calories per day. Your menu will support the detox process by including foods that are rich in phytochemicals, vitamins, minerals, healthy fats, and fiber. In addition to three smoothies a day, you can choose from a list of nutrient-dense snacks to ensure that you don't feel deprived.

The 3-day detox cleanse is not a fast, although you might be used to a higher calorie level. Because you may experience side effects such as fatigue or poor concentration, it is recommended that you begin your fast on a Friday so that the bulk of the detox happens over the weekend when you can stay home and take it easy. Detoxification requires you to slow down. If you have a fast-paced demanding job, you may want to consider taking a vacation day or planning a day with a light workload. Don't overschedule yourself for the weekend. Instead, allow yourself time and space to relax and rejuvenate. By the end of the 3-day detox cleanse, you will have built the foundations for a new routine and should feel confident to begin the 21-day plan.

10 COMMON DETOX SYMPTOMS
(AND HOW TO DEAL WITH THEM)

Before you begin the 3-day detox cleanse, you should be aware of some of the most common side effects associated with cleansing. Although unpleasant, they are just temporary and are signs that your body is eliminating toxins, which is good! Detox symptoms can occur for a number of reasons, the most prominent one being that when we eliminate processed foods, caffeine, alcohol, and sugar, we experience withdrawal-like symptoms.

Just like you would plan for a big trip, you will need to prepare and plan for the journey. You may find it helpful to keep a journal and use it as a way to keep track of the side effects you experience and note possible causes. Journaling during this phase is also a good tool for relieving emotional and mental stress.

The following sections describe some of the most common side effects that you may experience during the detox phase, why they occur, and what you can do to ease your symptoms.

1 **Headaches.** Headaches are one of the most common side effects of a detox, yet there is no clear cause. If you are a regular caffeine user, once you stop using it, withdrawal symptoms set in. Caffeine withdrawal is recognized as an official diagnosis based on research conducted by Johns Hopkins University (2004). The main symptoms include headaches of varying intensity along with irritability, fatigue, and depression. There is no clear scientific proof that sugar withdrawal causes headaches, however. Other potential reasons for headaches may include dehydration, hunger, and the removal of allergens, additives, excess salt, and preservatives from your diet.

Suggested remedy: According to the University of Maryland Medical Center (2014), headaches can be addressed a number of ways. Massage therapy can improve blood flow to the brain in order to ease the pain and tension. A technique to try is to use your fingertips and work them in a circular motion on your temples and forehead. Then rest your thumbs on each side of the bridge of your nose near your eyes right where it joins your forehead. Squeeze the bridge of your nose by applying firm pressure for about 10 seconds and repeat several times.

2 **Fatigue.** It is normal to experience fatigue during a cleanse, primarily due to the fact that you are probably eating fewer calories than you are used to.

Suggested remedy: Allow more time for rest and sleep. According to the Mayo Clinic (2014), adults should aim for seven to eight hours of uninterrupted sleep. Sleeping for less than seven hours a night is associated with a higher mortality rate and poorer performance on mental tasks. Including a 30-minute walk outside in the fresh air is a great way to boost energy. While you are outside, roll up your sleeves and let your skin soak up some natural vitamin D from the sun's rays.

3   **Bad Breath.** Bad breath is a common complaint for people who fast and is a symptom that you may experience as well. Digestive juices released in the absence of food begin to break down and affect the lining of the stomach, which can result in a foul odor. With insufficient saliva flowing to the mouth during times of reduced calorie intake, the mouth gets dry and bacteria from the tongue and teeth, which are normally taken care of with saliva, build up. This, along with the digestive juices, leads to a foul odor.

Suggested remedy: One of the best remedies for bad breath is to maintain good oral hygiene including tongue cleaning. Gently cleaning the tongue can include using a tongue scraper that you can pick up at the local drugstore. It is usually a U-shaped metal device that you hold at both ends and gently drag over the length of your tongue. Never scrap the underside of your tongue. Other ways to minimize bad breath are to floss regularly, brush frequently, and gargle with minty mouthwash.

4   **Frequent Urination.** During your cleanse you may notice that you are urinating more than usual. This is most likely a side effect of increasing the liquids in your diet as well as the result of toxins being eliminated from your body.

Suggested remedy: Continue to keep yourself hydrated, and if you feel as if you are urinating far too much, consider including an electrolyte drink into your day.

5   **Changes in Bowel Movements.** Changes in bowel habits are a common side effect, and some people may experience frequent loose stools and diarrhea, while others may find they are constipated. Diarrhea may be a flushing through of toxins that are in the cells of the GI (gastrointestinal) tract, as Dr. Amy Lanou, a nutrition scientist with the Physicians Committee for Responsible Medicine told *Today's Dietitian* in the May 2008 issue. Constipation is also a frequently experienced symptom and may be the result of the reduced volume of food in your GI tract.

Suggested remedy: For diarrhea, consider adding some of the suggested snacks that are bland and carbohydrate-based, such as whole-grain crackers. Keep yourself hydrated and consider adding an electrolyte drink. If you are constipated, try increasing the fiber content of your smoothies. Consider including a tablespoon of psyllium husk or ground flaxseed. Warm water with lemon and a brisk morning walk can also do the trick.

6 **Flatulence.** It is not uncommon to experience digestive discomfort when you change your diet. Vegetables and fruits contain soluble fiber and natural sugars like fructose that can produce excess gas in the small intestine.

Suggested remedy: Fortunately, there are several things that can help the embarrassment and discomfort from gas and bloating. Drink your smoothies slowly to prevent swallowing excess air and chew your snacks thoroughly. Consider drinking herbal teas including chamomile, ginger, peppermint, or fennel as each of these herbs can support healthy digestion. It will take your body time to adjust to the increase in fiber, but the symptoms should only be temporary.

7 **Intense Hunger and Cravings.** Hunger is one of the most difficult side effects to handle. You might experience it along with cravings during the first day of the cleanse as your body adjusts to reduced food consumption and less solid food.

Suggested remedy: Try to tune into your hunger and cravings. Determine whether you are physically hungry or experiencing a psychological desire to eat. Try distracting yourself by going for a walk, meditating, or drinking some water with lemon. If you are truly hungry, choose from the list of recommended snacks.

8 **Sleep Disturbances.** You may experience changes in sleep during the cleanse due to a combination of factors including low blood sugar, low fluids, withdrawal from various substances (e.g., sugar and caffeine), and even changes in your daily routine.

Suggested remedy: Allow yourself more time to rest during the cleanse. Engage in a sleep ritual such as turning off electronics an hour before bed, keeping your bedroom cool and dark, taking a hot bath, doing some gentle stretching, and drinking some herbal tea.

9 **Poor Concentration and Irritability.** The reduced caloric level and lessened amount of carbohydrates you are eating could lead to trouble concentrating as well as some irritability.

Suggested remedy: If you are experiencing light-headedness, then you should supplement your meals with the recommended snacks or bump up the ingredient portions in the smoothies.

10 **Runny Nose and Sneezing.** According to "Spring Cleaning: Assessing the Benefits and Risks of Detox Diets" in *Today's Dietitian* (2008), some people may get extreme runny noses or sneeze a lot. These symptoms may be the effects of the toxins moving out of the body, resulting in what feels like a strong allergy attack.

Suggested remedy: The symptoms should be temporary and resolve within the first day or two. Manage your symptoms by drinking plenty of fluids and getting additional rest. If you currently take medications for allergies, continue their use until you consult with your physician.

3-DAY MENU AT A GLANCE

Your 3-day detox cleanse includes three nutritionally balanced smoothies per day. Each smoothie includes ingredients that support digestive health and are rich in antioxidants, phytochemicals, and healthy fats. You shouldn't feel deprived or hungry while doing the cleanse, so if you find you need to eat between meals, choose from the list of healthy snacks included to supplement your diet. Your 3-day detox menu includes one green smoothie per day, which is made with only a little fruit or no fruit at all. Green smoothies are especially good for their cleansing properties and should leave your body feeling refreshed, clean, and energized.

	DAY 1	DAY 2	DAY 3
BREAKFAST	Fresh Start *(page 68)*	Goji Berry Breakfast *(page 73)*	Watermelon Cleanser *(page 76)*
LUNCH	Green Dreams *(page 69)*	Green Machine *(page 74)*	Tahini Teaser *(page 77)*
DINNER	Stomach Soother *(page 70)*	Apple Ginger Zinger *(page 75)*	Pineapple Turmeric Green Cleanser *(page 78)*

If you find you are overly hungry between meals, you may need a snack. Be moderate with your intake and keep your portions in check. The following is a list of 12 healthy plant-based snacks to choose from to incorporate throughout the plan:

1. Air-popped popcorn. Optional toppings: Nutritional yeast; Bragg's Liquid Amino Acids; drizzle of organic coconut oil or olive oil

2. Kale chips

3. Unsweetened, nondairy yogurt with fresh fruit

4. Edamame

5. Rice cakes with organic nut butter

6. Baked tofu

7. Vegetables and hummus (e.g., baby carrots, bell pepper strips, celery, broccoli florets)

8. Sliced tomatoes topped with a tablespoon of hemp seeds

9. Lightly thawed frozen cherries topped with sliced almonds

10. Apples, bananas, or celery with nut butter

11. Handful of unsalted nuts

12. Unsweetened dried fruit (e.g., dates, prunes, mango slices)

Having all of your ingredients prepped and ready to go will make your 3-day detox cleanse a breeze! For the majority of ingredients, you will simply need to measure out a portion right before you make your smoothie, but for others, there will be some prep that should be done in advance. Take a look at your schedule and book time the night before you begin your cleanse to prepare your ingredients. You may want to even set a reminder in your calendar so that you get an alert. Once you do your prep, your smoothie ingredients can be stored in small glass prep dishes or in zip-top bags and then placed in your refrigerator.

Day 1: Cook and slice your beet, and measure out ½ of an avocado.

Day 2: Measure out 2 tablespoons of Goji berries and place them in a small amount of water and refrigerate them until use. Dice your cucumber, chop your apple, grate 2 tablespoon of fresh ginger, and measure out ¼ cup of avocado.

Day 3: Chop 2 large celery sticks, measure out ½ of an avocado, juice 1 lemon, and grate 1 tablespoon of ginger. Labeling your containers or bags with the day and meal can make throwing the ingredients together fast and convenient.

SHOPPING LIST FOR THE 3-DAY CLEANSE

Before you start your cleanse, plan on taking a shopping trip to purchase all of the ingredients that you will need. For some of them, you will have extra left over. The bulk sections of most grocery stores carry the nuts and seeds that you will need, which will allow you to only purchase the required quantity. If you don't have a bulk section, you still shouldn't need to worry about waste as each of the ingredients in the cleanse will also be used in the 21-day plan. You can also use any of the ingredients as substitutions or additions to any of the recipes based on your personal preferences. Remember, two variations are listed with each recipe.

The shopping list encompasses the four following groups.

FRESH PRODUCE

Fresh vegetables
1 organic red beet
2 medium avocados
1 bunch celery
1 small cucumber

Fresh fruit
1 (8-ounce) container cubed watermelon
1 (8-ounce) container cubed pineapple
1 green apple
1 lemon

Fresh herbs
1 bunch mint
1 bunch parsley
4-inch piece of fresh ginger root

FROZEN AISLE

Frozen vegetables
1 (8-ounce) bag frozen broccoli
1 (16-ounce) bag frozen spinach
1 (16-ounce) bag frozen kale

Frozen fruit
1 (10-ounce) bag frozen mango
1 (10-ounce) bag frozen cherries
1 (10-ounce) bag frozen blueberries
1 (10-ounce) bag frozen raspberries
1 (10-ounce) bag frozen papaya
1 (10-ounce) bag frozen cranberries

DAIRY

1 quart unsweetened vanilla or plain almond milk
1 quart unsweetened, protein-fortified almond milk with added protein. A suggested brand is So Delicious Almond Plus 5X.
1 (6-ounce) container plain unsweetened coconut or almond yogurt

PANTRY

1 (8-ounce) bag rolled oats (not quick oats)
1 (8-ounce) package ground flaxseed
1 (8-ounce) package hemp seeds
1 (8-ounce) package chia seeds
1 (4-ounce) package psyllium husk. You can find the husk in most bulk sections so you can purchase a small quantity.

Dried fruit
3 Medjool dates
1 (4-ounce) package dried Goji berries
1 (4-ounce) package unsweetened cacao

Nuts
4 ounces pumpkin seeds
4 ounces raw cashews

Dried herbs
Ground cinnamon
Ground turmeric
One jar of unsweetened sesame tahini

FRESH START

HIGH-FIBER • PROTEIN-PACKED

Start your cleanse with an energizing smoothie made with cleansing beets, antioxidant-rich cherries, and cacao. The hemp seeds provide healthy omega-3 fats and protein to keep you feeling satisfied.

Tip: One serving of hemp seeds (2 to 3 tablespoons) contains 10 grams of plant-based protein and 10 grams of omega fats in addition to 3 grams of fiber, B vitamins, iron, and zinc.

1 cup unsweetened vanilla almond milk

2 tablespoons hemp seeds

¼ cup rolled oats

¾ cup frozen cherries

1 medium beet, cooked and sliced

1 teaspoon unsweetened cacao

1 cup ice

In a blender, combine the almond milk, hemp seeds, and oats and blend into a thick paste. Add the remaining ingredients and blend until smooth. Serve right away.

VARIATION 1: If beets aren't your thing, substitute ½ a green apple.

VARIATION 2: For extra flavor, grate 1 tablespoon of orange rind into the blender.

Nutritional info: calories: 423, fat: 17 grams, carbs: 50 grams, fiber: 10 grams, protein: 16 grams

"If you think you can do a thing or think you can't do a thing, you are right." —HENRY FORD

INTENTION
Today I will give myself permission to slow down.

GREEN DREAMS

HIGH-FIBER • HEART-HEALTHY

Broccoli may seem like an unusual smoothie ingredient, but the bitterness is tempered by the addition of the flavorful berries. The health benefits of this smoothie are off the charts with high levels of vitamins A and C, folate, fiber, monounsaturated fats, and omega-3 fats.

Tip: Avocados are rich in monounsaturated fats and can increase feelings of satiety.

1 cup unsweetened, protein-fortified almond milk

2 tablespoons ground flaxseed

1 Medjool date, pitted

½ cup avocado

1 cup frozen spinach

½ cup frozen broccoli

½ cup frozen blueberries

1 cup ice

In a blender, combine the almond milk, flaxseed, date, and avocado and process into a thick paste. Add the remaining ingredients and blend until smooth. If the smoothie is too thick, add more liquid and thin to desired consistency. Serve right away.

VARIATION 1: Substitute the almond milk with coconut kefir.

VARIATION 2: Add ¼ cup diced tofu for extra protein.

Nutritional info: calories: 390, fat: 19 grams, carbs: 36 grams, fiber: 18 grams, protein: 12 grams

STOMACH SOOTHER

HIGH-FIBER • PROTEIN-PACKED

Nourish your digestive system with the power of probiotics and natural enzymes. Papaya contains the digestive enzyme papain, as well as fiber and vitamins A and C. It also adds a buttery consistency and sweet taste.

Tip: Probiotics in cultured products promote the growth of beneficial bacteria in your GI tract.

8 to 12 ounces water

2 tablespoons chia seeds

¼ cup raw cashews

1 (6-ounce) container plain coconut yogurt

1 cup frozen papaya

1 sprig mint

1 cup ice

In a blender, combine the water, chia seeds, and cashews and process into a thick paste. Add the remaining ingredients and blend until smooth. Serve right away.

VARIATION 1: Substitute the coconut yogurt with almond yogurt or coconut kefir.

VARIATION 2: Use almond milk instead of water for extra richness.

Nutritional info: calories: 484, fat: 27 grams, carbs: 56 grams, fiber: 15 grams, protein: 23 grams

GOJI BERRY BREAKFAST

HIGH-FIBER · HEART-HEALTHY · PROTEIN-PACKED · BRAIN-BOOSTING

The cranberry-sized Goji berry is truly in a league of its own and is packed with antioxidants and vitamin C. Their mild, tangy taste mingles with the sweet and sour flavors of the other berries, making this anti-inflammatory, antioxidant-rich smoothie a great go-to breakfast.

Tip: The phytochemicals in berries can reduce the risk for chronic diseases like diabetes, cancer, and heart disease.

1 cup unsweetened vanilla almond milk

2 tablespoons hemp seeds

¼ cup rolled oats

2 tablespoons Goji berries, soaked in water for 15 minutes

½ cup frozen blueberries

½ cup frozen raspberries

½ cup frozen cranberries

1 cup ice

In a blender, combine the almond milk, hemp seeds, and oats and process into a thick paste. Add the remaining ingredients and blend until smooth. Serve right away.

VARIATION 1: Substitute the rolled oats with 2 tablespoons of coconut flour. Both are used to provide thickness and slow-burning carbs.

VARIATION 2: Add the zest of one lemon to bring out the "tang" in the berries.

Nutritional info: calories: 400, fat: 14 grams, carbs: 43 grams, fiber: 12 grams, protein: 17 grams

"Obstacles are those frightful things you see when you take your eyes off your goal." —HENRY FORD

INTENTION
Today I will be grateful.

GREEN MACHINE

JOINT-SUPPORTING • BEAUTY-BOOSTING

Hydrate and boost your immune system with this green smoothie. Pumpkin seeds are high in immune-boosting zinc and blood-building iron, two minerals that can be tricky to get enough of in your diet. This energy booster is also high in magnesium and vitamin C and is bursting with antioxidants.

Tip: Cucumbers are very low in calories and high in water and can keep you hydrated.

1 cup unsweetened vanilla almond milk

¼ cup pumpkin seeds

¼ cup avocado

1 cup frozen kale

1 small cucumber

¼ cup parsley

1 Medjool date, pitted

1 cup ice

In a blender, combine the almond milk and pumpkin seeds and process into a thick paste. Add the remaining ingredients and blend until smooth. Serve right away.

VARIATION 1: Substitute the avocado with tofu.

VARIATION 2: Add ½ cup frozen blueberries.

Nutritional info: calories: 400, fat: 23 grams, carbs: 39 grams, fiber: 10 grams, protein: 15 grams

APPLE GINGER ZINGER

JOINT-SUPPORTING • HEART-HEALTHY • HIGH-FIBER

Prepare your body for restful sleep with a smoothie made of melatonin-rich cherries and digestion-promoting ginger. The added slow-burning carbohydrates from the oats and the protein from the milk make this smoothie a tasty sleep-inducing nightcap.

Tip: Ginger root is good for digestion and acts as an anti-inflammatory.

1 cup unsweetened, protein-fortified almond milk

2 tablespoons ground flaxseed

1 medium apple, cored and chopped

¾ cup frozen cherries

1 tablespoon chopped ginger root

¼ cup rolled oats

1 cup ice

In a blender, combine the almond milk and flaxseed and process into a thick paste. Add the remaining ingredients and blend until smooth. Serve right away.

VARIATION 1: Substitute the high-protein almond milk with soymilk.

VARIATION 2: Add 6 ounces of vanilla-flavored soy or coconut yogurt.

Nutritional info: calories: 380, fat: 8 grams, carbs: 62 grams, fiber: 15 grams, protein: 11 grams

WATERMELON CLEANSER

HIGH-FIBER • PROTEIN-PACKED

Start the last day of your cleanse with this detoxifying combination. This smoothie contains the underrated celery plant, which provides antioxidant and anti-inflammatory factors along with pectin for digestive-tract support. The urinary tract benefits of cranberries and the hydrating effects of watermelon make this smoothie a winning cleanser.

Tip: Watermelon is low in calories and rich in the phytochemical lycopene, which may protect against heart disease and cancer.

1 cup unsweetened, protein-fortified almond milk

½ cup frozen cranberries

2 large celery stalks, chopped

1 cup diced watermelon

1 cup frozen spinach

2 tablespoons ground flaxseed

½ cup rolled oats

1 cup ice

In a blender, combine all of the ingredients and blend until smooth. Serve right away.

VARIATION 1: Substitute the almond milk with coconut yogurt.

VARIATION 2: Add fresh mint or parsley as additional digestive aids.

Nutritional info: calories: 400, fat: 11 grams, carbs: 54 grams, fiber: 17 grams, protein: 22 grams

"Believe you can and you are halfway there." —THEODORE ROOSEVELT

INTENTION
Today I will reflect on my 3-day cleanse.

TAHINI TEASER

HIGH-FIBER • JOINT-SUPPORTING • PROTEIN-PACKED

You may think of hummus when you see tahini, but the combination of tahini with vanilla, fruits, and a date will satisfy your sweet tooth while providing long-lasting energy to prevent the dreaded 3 p.m. slump. The added cinnamon gives this rich-tasting smoothie warm undertones.

Tip: Sesame tahini is rich in mono-unsaturated fats, vitamins, minerals, and phytochemicals. A 2-tablespoon serving has 10 percent of the daily value of iron, 25 percent of magnesium, 22 percent of phosphorus, 21 percent of copper, 20 percent of manganese and zinc, and 30 percent thiamin!

1 cup unsweetened vanilla almond milk

1 cup frozen kale

2 tablespoons sesame tahini

½ cup frozen raspberries

½ cup frozen mangos

1 tablespoon hemp seeds

1 Medjool date, pitted

½ teaspoon ground cinnamon

1 cup ice

In a blender, combine all of the ingredients and blend until smooth. Serve right away.

VARIATION 1: Substitute the hemp seeds with chia seeds.

VARIATION 2: Add ¼ cup rolled oats for extra thickness and slow-burning carbs.

Nutritional info: calories: 456, fat: 24 grams, carbs: 48 grams, fiber: 11 grams, protein: 15 grams

PINEAPPLE TURMERIC GREEN CLEANSER

JOINT-SUPPORTING • HIGH-FIBER

This cleansing smoothie is made from pineapple, which contains bromelain, a type of natural digestive enzyme, and the spices ginger and turmeric, powerful anti-inflammatories. Lemon has an alkalizing effect on the body and acts as a natural diuretic, helping you eliminate excess fluid.

Tip: Psyllium husk is a soluble fiber than can lower cholesterol and ease symptoms of diarrhea and constipation.

⅛ cup raw cashews

1 cup unsweetened, protein-fortified almond milk

½ cup avocado

1 cup chopped fresh pineapple

1 cup frozen kale

½ cup frozen broccoli

Juice of ½ lemon

1 tablespoon pysllium husk

1 tablespoon grated fresh ginger

¼ teaspoon ground turmeric

1 cup ice

In a blender, combine the cashews with the milk and process into a paste. Add the remaining ingredients and blend until smooth. Serve right away.

VARIATION 1: Substitute the cashews with Brazil nuts.

VARIATION 2: To bump up the diuretic properties, add ½ cup sliced beet, celery, or cucumber.

Nutritional info: calories: 380, fat: 19 grams, carbs: 40 grams, fiber: 14 grams, protein: 14 grams

You did it! Congratulations on completing your 3-day detox cleanse! By reviewing and renewing your food intake over the last three days, you should feel empowered, motivated, and ready to continue with your healthy habits. By nourishing your body with whole foods rich in phyto-chemicals, antioxidants, omega-3 fatty acids, and plant-based proteins, you should feel energized and recharged. To help you continue your journey to improved health and new habits, you are encouraged to continue with the 21-day plan. Each day of the plan will include one healthy smoothie recipe for you to use as a meal replacement or hearty snack. In addition to the main smoothie recipe, there will be a suggested salad recipe to include in your day.

NOTES

CHAPTER 5

WEEK 1

As you start Week 1 of the healthy smoothie plan, you should feel a sense of accomplishment that you were able to break your old cycle of eating, rid your body of processed foods, and nourish yourself with a nutrient-dense, plant-based diet. You may find that your cravings have decreased, your bowel habits are better, and your taste buds are looking forward to more delicious fresh fruits and vegetables.

While detoxifications are not meant to be long-term solutions to weight problems, they can be effective motivators for making healthy dietary changes, such as eating more fruits and vegetables and increasing dietary fiber intake. Unfortunately, when Monday morning rolls around, you may find it comforting to go back to your old routines of consuming vending-machine food and late-night takeout. For lasting weight loss, it is what you do after the cleanse period that ends up affecting your overall body weight. For the next three weeks, you will be able to practice your new habits by replacing one meal a day with one nutrient-dense smoothie. The plan will also include a list of recommended salads that you can include with the smoothie or as one of your other meals. Perfection is not the goal, but rather aim to do a little more and a little better each day. Slip-ups are natural, especially if clean eating is new to you, so be gentle on yourself and celebrate each small success. Along with healthy eating, try to be active every single day, if possible, for at least thirty minutes.

MENU AT A GLANCE

	SMOOTHIE	SUGGESTED SALAD
MONDAY	Get Your Green On (page 86)	Spinach Asparagus Salad (page 159)
TUESDAY	Peanut Butter and Jelly (page 89)	Kale Cucumber Salad (page 146)
WEDNESDAY	Mango Coconut (page 90)	Black Bean and Tofu Salad (page 146)
THURSDAY	Raspberry Turmeric (page 93)	Edamame Salad (page 150)
FRIDAY	Almond Date Cacao (page 94)	Power Salad (page 156)
SATURDAY	Green Tea and Mango (page 97)	Cannellini Bean Salad (page 150)
SUNDAY	Vanilla Chai (page 98)	Lentil Cauliflower Salad (page 154)

One of the best ways to ensure success is to set yourself up for it! You have the power to build healthy new eating habits by taking charge of your kitchen. Many people find it useful to do a pantry clean-out in order to remove foods that don't really fit into a healthy-eating plan. Set aside a couple of hours on the weekend to go through your pantry, cupboards, freezer, and refrigerator. Remove highly processed foods and "junk" and donate it to a local food bank or homeless shelter. You will need the space for the nutritious ingredients that are used in the smoothie recipes and salads. Nothing makes healthy eating easier than an organized kitchen stocked with nutrient-dense foods.

Here is a list of pantry staples that you should keep on hand.

- Canned beans
- Nut butters
- Rolled oats
- Raw nuts and seeds: cashew, pumpkin, almond, hemp, ground flaxseed, chia
- Frozen fruit: mango, cherries, berries
- Frozen vegetables: spinach, kale, broccoli
- Shelf-stable almond milk
- Silken tofu, firm tofu
- Refrigerated almond milk, coconut milk
- Coconut water
- Unsweetened cacao
- Medjool dates
- Teas: green tea, chai tea
- Canned pumpkin

PREP

Healthy eating isn't difficult, but it does take a little prep time. For the majority of smoothies, you will simply need to read the recipe through before starting. Most of the recipes will require nothing more than measuring out your ingredients, tossing them in the blender, blending, and enjoying! However, there are a few items that should be prepped in advance so that you can just grab 'n' go. Make it a habit to set aside time on Sunday afternoon or evening to prepare your ingredients for the week. You may find it helpful to set a recurring reminder on your phone.

Fresh produce: Cook, cool, slice, and refrigerate 1 medium beet; slice a banana and portion into two bags and freeze; slice an avocado and measure out ¼ cup.

Pantry: Open a can of pumpkin, measure out ½ cup, and store the remainder in the refrigerator as an add-in to other recipes or to stir into oats or yogurt. Pumpkin can also be stored in the freezer.

Liquids: Brew a cup of green tea and a cup of chai tea, cool, and store in the refrigerator until ready to use.

Dairy: Measure out 1 cup of silken tofu. The remainder can be frozen in ½- or 1-cup portions or used in the suggested salads.

WEEK 1 SHOPPING LIST

SMOOTHIE SHOPPING LIST

To prepare the smoothies for Week 1, you will need the following ingredients:

Dairy

1 quart unsweetened vanilla almond milk
    or coconut milk
1 (11-ounce) container coconut water
1 (14-ounce) package water-packed silken tofu
1 (6-ounce) containers vanilla soy yogurt
1 (6-ounce) container coconut yogurt

Frozen aisle

1 (16-ounce) package kale
1 (16-ounce) package spinach
1½ cups raspberries
2 cups mango
1 cup cherries

Fresh produce

1 banana
1 avocado
1 lime
1 red beet
1 bunch mint
2-inch piece ginger root

Pantry

3 tablespoons ground flaxseed
2 tablespoons chia seeds
4 tablespoons hemp seeds
1 tablespoon unsweetened cacao
½ cup rolled oats
1 tablespoon peanut butter
1 tablespoon almond butter
1 tablespoon sesame tahini
2 Medjool dates
½ cup canned pumpkin

Spices

Ground turmeric
Ground cinnamon
Vanilla extract

SUGGESTED SALADS SHOPPING LIST

There are seven suggested salad recipes that accompany the seven smoothie recipes. They are all plant-based, nutritionally balanced, highly customizable, and quick to throw together. To prepare the salads, you should purchase the following ingredients:

Fresh produce

1 bunch fresh kale
1 bunch fresh spinach
1 (16-ounce) container salad greens
1 red bell pepper
Grape tomatoes
Shredded carrots
Thinly shredded cabbage
Button mushrooms
1 medium avocado
1 bunch baby broccoli stalks
Small head of cauliflower
Pea shoots
Alfalfa sprouts
1 cup shelled edamame
1 cup sugar snap peas
2 cups fresh green beans
1 teaspoon grated ginger
1 bunch fresh cilantro

Pantry

1 jar water-packed artichoke hearts
1 jar oil-packed sun-dried tomatoes
1 can cannellini beans
1 can black beans
1 can garbanzo beans
1 can lentils
1 tablespoon pumpkin seeds
1 tablespoon sunflower seeds

Dairy (can often be found in produce)

1 cup crumbled firm tofu

GET YOUR GREEN ON

HIGH-PROTEIN

This green smoothie is high in healthy omega-3 and monounsaturated fats, vitamins A and C, folate, and fiber. The mint will stimulate your digestion, while the high protein content will keep you feeling full and satisfied for hours.

Tip: Try freezing the avocado and tofu to make your smoothie extra thick.

1 cup silken tofu

2 tablespoons ground flaxseed

1 cup frozen kale

¼ cup avocado

½ frozen banana

1 tablespoon fresh mint

1 cup ice

In a blender, combine all of the ingredients and blend until smooth. Serve right away.

VARIATION 1: Substitute the tofu with soy yogurt.

VARIATION 2: Add a serving of protein powder.

Nutritional info: calories: 330, fat: 15 grams, carbs: 28 grams, fiber: 10 grams, protein: 16 grams

SALAD PAIRING: SPINACH ASPARAGUS SALAD, PAGE 159

"With the new day comes new strength and new thoughts." —ELEANOR ROOSEVELT

INTENTION
Today I will focus on eating slowly.

PEANUT BUTTER AND JELLY

HIGH-PROTEIN

A healthy version of a classic favorite, this peanut butter and "jelly" smoothie is full of slow-burning carbs and plant-based protein. Nutrient-rich raspberries take the place of sugar-filled jelly. As an added benefit, the chia seeds give this smoothie an extra dose of fiber and omega-3 fats.

Tip: Soak your chia seeds in a small amount of water in the refrigerator for 10 to 15 minutes. They will form a gel and add extra thickness to your smoothie.

1 cup unsweetened vanilla almond milk

½ cup frozen raspberries

1 tablespoon peanut butter

1 tablespoon chia seeds

½ cup rolled oats

1 cup ice

In a blender, combine all of the ingredients and blend until smooth. Serve right away.

VARIATION 1: Substitute almond butter for peanut butter.

VARIATION 2: Add 6 ounces of soy yogurt.

Nutritional info: calories: 355, fat: 17 grams, carbs: 36 grams, fiber: 12 grams, protein: 13 grams

SALAD PAIRING: KALE CUCUMBER SALAD, PAGE 146

"Setting goals is the first step in turning the invisible into the visible." —TONY ROBBINS

INTENTION

Today I will be mindful of my hunger and fullness cues.

MANGO COCONUT

HIGH-FIBER

Mangos are high in vitamin C, vitamin B_6, vitamin A, potassium, pectin, and soluble fibers. This "king of fruits" can keep your cholesterol in check and your digestive system running smoothly.

Tip: Mango has pectin, a type of soluble fiber that can help lower "bad" cholesterol.

1 (11-ounce) container coconut water

1 (6-ounce) container vanilla coconut yogurt

1 cup frozen mango

1 tablespoon sesame tahini

1 tablespoon lime juice

1 cup ice

In a blender, combine all of the ingredients and blend until smooth. Serve right away.

VARIATION 1: Substitute coconut milk for the coconut water.

VARIATION 2: Add 2 tablespoons coconut flour to increase the fiber content and for added thickness.

Nutritional info: calories: 380, fat: 16 grams, carbs: 56 grams, fiber: 4 grams, protein: 5 grams

SALAD PAIRING: BLACK BEAN AND TOFU SALAD, PAGE 146

"Physical fitness is not only one of the most important keys to a healthy body, it is the basis of dynamic and creative intellectual activity." —JOHN F. KENNEDY

INTENTION

Today I will be active for 30 minutes.

RASPBERRY TURMERIC

JOINT SUPPORT

Inflammation is part of your body's immune response, but when it is out of control from poor eating habits, it can lead to joint pain, cancer, and heart disease. Beets, berries, omega-3 fats from the hemp seeds, and turmeric make this smoothie a winning inflammation fighter. Not your typical smoothie ingredient, the peppery, warm flavor of turmeric adds a bit of spice and earthiness.

Tip: Turmeric has long been used in Chinese and Indian medicine as an anti-inflammatory to treat a wide variety of conditions.

1 cup unsweetened vanilla almond milk

¾ cup frozen raspberries

1 medium cooked beet, sliced

½ frozen banana

2 tablespoons hemp seeds

¼ teaspoon ground turmeric

1 cup ice

In a blender, combine all of the ingredients and blend until smooth. Serve right away.

VARIATION 1: Substitute silken tofu for the almond milk for added anti-inflammatory factors.

VARIATION 2: Add 1 cup frozen spinach to boost the vitamin A and C content even further.

Nutritional info: calories: 354, fat: 16 grams, carbs: 40 grams, fiber: 13 grams, protein: 13 grams

SALAD PAIRING: EDAMAME SALAD, PAGE 150

"Pursue one great decisive aim with force and determination."

—CARL VON CLAUSEWITZ

INTENTION

Today I will go outside in nature for 10 to 15 minutes.

ALMOND DATE CACAO

HEART-HEALTHY • BRAIN-BOOSTING

This rich-tasting chocolaty smoothie serves up high levels of antioxidants from the cherries and cacao and healthy fats and vitamin E from the almonds. All three foods are considered to be heart healthy due to their ability to reduce cholesterol, keep your blood vessels healthy, and reduce inflammation.

Tip: Almonds make a great filling snack. A 1-ounce serving, about 23 kernels, has just 160 calories, 14 grams of fat, 3 grams of fiber, and 6 grams of protein.

1 cup unsweetened vanilla almond milk

1 tablespoon unsweetened cacao

1 cup frozen cherries

1 tablespoon almond butter

1 Medjool date, pitted

1 cup ice

In a blender, combine all of the ingredients and blend until smooth. Serve right away.

VARIATION 1: Substitute yogurt or tofu for the almond milk.

VARIATION 2: Add 2 tablespoons ground flaxseed for omega-3 fats and fiber.

Nutritional info: calories: 371, fat: 19 grams, carbs: 50 grams, fiber: 9 grams, protein: 7 grams

SALAD PAIRING: POWER SALAD, PAGE 156

"Knowing is not enough; we must apply. Willing is not enough; we must do."
—JOHANN WOLFGANG VON GOETHE

INTENTION
Today I will be calm.

GREEN TEA AND MANGO

BRAIN-BOOSTING

This smoothie will give you good clean energy that won't result in a crash. Rev up your metabolism with a smoothie made using antioxidant-rich green tea and stay satisfied for hours with plant-based hemp seed protein.

Tip: One cup of green tea has about 35mg of caffeine compared to 8 ounces of brewed coffee, which contains about 200mg of caffeine.

1 cup brewed and cooled green tea

1 (6-ounce) container of plain yogurt

1 cup frozen mango

1 cup frozen spinach

2 tablespoons hemp seeds

1 to 2 Medjool dates, pitted

1 cup ice

In a blender, combine all of the ingredients and blend until smooth. Serve right away.

VARIATION 1: Substitute yogurt or tofu for the almond milk.

VARIATION 2: Add ¼ cup rolled oats for additional slow-burning carbs.

Nutritional info: calories: 371, fat: 19 grams, carbs: 50 grams, fiber: 9 grams, protein: 7 grams

SALAD PAIRING: CANNELLINI BEAN SALAD, PAGE 150

"With the new day comes new strengths and new thoughts." —ELEANOR ROOSEVELT

INTENTION

Today I will be content.

VANILLA CHAI

LOW-CALORIE • BRAIN-BOOSTING • JOINT SUPPORT

Warm up with this spicy, antioxidant-rich smoothie made with low-calorie, nutrient-rich pumpkin. One cup of pumpkin has less than 50 calories and 3 grams of fiber so it can keep you full longer on fewer calories. One serving of this smoothie will also give you almost 200 percent of your recommended daily intake of vitamin A and a hefty dose of antioxidants.

Tip: The spices used in chai mixes are rich in antioxidants and are known for their anti-inflammatory benefits.

1 cup brewed and cooled chai tea

1 (6-ounce) container vanilla soy yogurt

½ cup canned pumpkin

1 tablespoon chia seeds

1 tablespoon ground flaxseed

½ teaspoon vanilla extract

1 cup ice

In a blender, combine all of the ingredients and blend until smooth. Serve right away.

VARIATION 1: If you don't have chai tea, use water and the following spices: ½ teaspoon powdered ginger, ½ teaspoon ground cinnamon, and a dash each of cardamom, cloves, and nutmeg.

VARIATION 2: Add ½ cup diced red apple for additional heart-healthy fiber and sweetness.

Nutritional info: calories: 290, fat: 10 grams, carbs: 40 grams, fiber: 12 grams, protein: 11 grams

SALAD PAIRING: LENTIL CAULIFLOWER SALAD, PAGE 154

"What you do today can improve all your tomorrows." —RALPH MARSTON

INTENTION
Today I will be loving.

WEEKLY WRAP-UP

WEEK 1

Congratulations on completing Week 1 of your healthy smoothie plan! By the end of this week, you should start noticing some changes in your energy level and digestion. You may feel yourself thinking more clearly or sleeping better. If weight loss is a goal, you may even have lost a pound or two. But if things didn't go as well as you expected or if your car went on autopilot and took you through the drive-thru, don't get discouraged. Change takes time, and old habits are hard to break. The most important thing is to be kind to yourself, celebrate each small success, and take each day as a new beginning. Next week you will have the chance to continue to practice your new skills and habits by trying out a whole new mix of delicious, nourishing smoothie recipes.

NOTES

CHAPTER 6

WEEK 2

Welcome to Week 2 of your 21-day healthy smoothie plan! This week you will be presented with seven more unique and nourishing smoothie recipes and suggested salads. Two of the smoothies each week are green smoothies that contain little or no fruit. All of the smoothies are nutritionally balanced with healthy fats; slow-burning, high-fiber carbohydrates; nutritionally dense fruits and vegetables; and plant-based protein.

By this point, blending up a healthy drink should be easier than at first and feel more natural as part of your healthy lifestyle. You might notice how the different foods make you feel and also tune into your hunger and fullness cues more deeply. Each chapter has a section for you to record notes, such as smoothies that made you feel particularly energized or ones that kept you full for hours.

Remember physical activity! Following a healthy diet is only part of the equation, so make time each day to be active. Aim for 30 minutes most days and make it something you enjoy: Take a walk in the park, ride your bike, do yoga, or go for a swim or run. Consider setting two to three specific goals for being active to go along with your healthy-eating plan and kick your health up another notch this week!

MENU AT A GLANCE

	SMOOTHIE	SUGGESTED SALAD
MONDAY	Green Pear-fection *(page 106)*	The Simple Vegan Salad *(page 158)*
TUESDAY	Mocha Cashew *(page 109)*	A Taste of Italy Salad *(page 161)*
WEDNESDAY	Pumpkin Power *(page 110)*	Black Bean Mango Salad *(page 148)*
THURSDAY	Dandelion Green *(page 113)*	Raw Slaw Salad *(page 158)*
FRIDAY	Raspberry Almond *(page 114)*	The Middle Eastern Salad *(page 155)*
SATURDAY	Berry Blue Tea *(page 117)*	Lentil Beet Salad *(page 153)*
SUNDAY	Orange Creamsicle *(page 118)*	Hoppin' John Salad *(page 151)*

Before the week begins, do a pantry, freezer, and refrigerator review and make a list of ingredients that you are low on. The smoothie recipes and salads in this book mix and match many core ingredients in order to limit the number of items that you need to purchase. However, feel free to substitute ingredients based on your personal preferences and tastes. For example, cashews can be replaced by walnuts, peanut and almond butters with sunflower seed butter, dates with frozen banana, pumpkin with sweet potato, kale with collard greens, and cherries with blueberries. You get the idea. If you are missing an ingredient, don't let that stop you from trying out a recipe. Use the information in the previous chapters to find a suitable substitution, and let your creativity and imagination run wild! The combinations are literally endless.

The majority of the ingredients for the smoothies can simply be measured and tossed into the blender. However, to save time and make blending fast and convenient, allot time on Sunday to read through each recipe and prep and store the following ingredients:

Fresh produce: Chop one medium pear; measure and store ¼ cup of avocado; slice ½ cup of jicama; cut one medium banana in half and slice each half into quarter-size rounds, place in a zip-top bag and freeze; grate 1 tablespoon of fresh ginger; and wash and refrigerate 1 cup of dandelion greens.

Dairy: Portion your silken tofu into two ½-cup servings.

Liquids: Brew a cup of coffee, chill, and refrigerate, and brew a cup of rooibos tea, chill, and refrigerate.

Nuts and seeds: You might like the added thickness that results from soaking your seeds and nuts before blending. If so, portion out two 1½-tablespoon servings of hemp seeds, 1 tablespoon of chia seeds, and 2 tablespoons of cashews. Place each in a small amount of water and refrigerate.

WEEK 2 SHOPPING LIST

SMOOTHIE SHOPPING LIST

To prepare the seven smoothies in Week 2 of your healthy smoothie plan, you will need the following ingredients:

Dairy
1 quart unsweetened vanilla almond milk (you will need 3 cups total)
3 (6-ounce) containers vanilla soy yogurt
1 cup silken tofu
8 ounces orange juice

Pantry
1 (11-ounce) carton of coconut water
Coffee for brewing
Rooibos tea bags
Seeds: 3 tablespoons ground flaxseed, 3 tablespoons hemp seeds, 1 tablespoon chia seeds
Nuts: 2 tablespoons raw cashews
Dried fruit: 2 Medjool dates, 2 tablespoons Goji berries
1 tablespoon unsweetened cacao
1 graham cracker square
½ cup canned pumpkin
1 tablespoon almond butter
2 tablespoons rolled oats

Fresh produce
Fresh vegetables: ½ cup shelled edamame, 1 cup dandelion greens, ½ cup jicama
Fresh fruit: 1 medium pear, ¼ cup avocado, 1 banana, 1 lime
1 teaspoon grated ginger

Frozen aisle
Frozen vegetables: 1 cup kale, 1 cup spinach
Frozen fruit: ¾ cup cherries, ½ cup cranberries, ¾ cup raspberries, 1 cup mango, 1 cup blueberries

Spices
Pumpkin pie spice
Ground cinnamon
Vanilla extract

SUGGESTED SALADS SHOPPING LIST

There are seven suggested salads to go along with the smoothie recipes (see Chapter 8, pages 143 to 163, for recipes). The salads are simple and quick to prepare and include plant-based protein, healthy fats, and at least three or more servings of fruits and vegetables. Some of the same ingredients that are used in the smoothies are also called for in the salads in order to simplify your shopping and prep.

To prepare the suggested salads, you will need the following ingredients:

Fresh produce
Mixed salad greens: 10 cups
Fresh vegetables: 1 cup sugar snap peas, 1 green pepper, 1 red bell pepper, 1 onion, 1 container grape tomatoes, 1 package shredded coleslaw, 1 package shredded carrots, 1 bunch baby broccoli, 1 bunch asparagus spears, ½ cup edamame, 1 container pea shoots, 4 large tomatoes, 1 cup green beans, 1 container alfalfa sprouts, 1 medium beet, 1 cup mushrooms, ½ cup jicama
Fresh fruit: ½ mango, ½ avocado
Fresh herbs: basil, mint, fennel, cilantro

Dairy
1 (15-ounce) container firm tofu
1 package baked tofu
1 container hummus

Breads
1 whole-grain pita pocket

Pantry
Canned/jarred vegetables: artichoke hearts, black olives
Nuts and seeds: 2 tablespoons peanuts, 1 tablespoon pumpkin seeds
Canned beans: ½ cup black-eyed peas, ½ cup black beans, 1 cup lentils

GREEN PEAR-FECTION

BEAUTY-BOOSTING · HIGH-PROTEIN · HIGH-FIBER

Start your week on an energizing note with this green smoothie featuring skin-nourishing pears and plant-based protein. Pears are ranked as one of the most easily digested fruits and are also considered to be a low-allergy food. The skin of this fruit contains an array of phytochemicals and about half of the pear's fiber, so leave it on for maximum nutritional benefits.

Tip: Edamame contains phytoestrogens that can reduce the risk for chronic diseases and, when blended, lend a creamy consistency.

1 cup unsweetened vanilla almond milk

1 cup frozen kale

½ cup shelled edamame

1 medium pear, diced

2 tablespoons ground flaxseed

1 teaspoon grated fresh ginger

1 cup ice

In a blender, combine all of the ingredients and blend until smooth. Serve right away.

VARIATION 1: Substitute yogurt or tofu for the almond milk.

VARIATION 2: Add 2 tablespoons shelled hemp seed to boost the omega-3 and protein content.

Nutritional info: calories: 341, fat: 11 grams, carbs: 47 grams, fiber: 16 grams, protein: 16 grams

SALAD PAIRING: THE SIMPLE VEGAN SALAD, PAGE 158

"Knowledge is power."
—SIR FRANCIS BACON

INTENTION
Today I will take care of my body.

MOCHA CASHEW

BRAIN-BOOSTING • HEART-HEALTHY

Coffee is more than just a vehicle for caffeine. With or without caffeine, coffee is rich in biologically active components that may reduce one's risk for developing Parkinson's and Alzheimer's disease and certain types of cancer. In a blender, combined with the rich taste of cashews and cacao, this is one fancy coffee smoothie that you won't feel guilty about drinking.

Tip: *Medjool dates are used to provide natural sweetness and added thickness.*

2 tablespoons raw cashews

1 Medjool date, pitted

1 cup brewed and cooled coffee
   (regular or decaffeinated)

1 (6-ounce) container vanilla soy yogurt

1 tablespoon unsweetened cacao

¾ cup frozen cherries

½ teaspoon vanilla extract

1 cup ice

In a blender, add the cashews and date and process into a paste. Combine the remaining ingredients and blend until smooth. Serve right away.

VARIATION 1: Substitute unsweetened cocoa for the cacao. Both of them are rich in antioxidants.

VARIATION 2: Add 1 serving of protein powder.

Nutritional info: calories: 443, fat: 19 grams, carbs: 76 grams, fiber: 8 grams, protein: 11 grams

SALAD PAIRING: A TASTE OF ITALY SALAD, PAGE 161

"You are never too old to set another goal or to dream a new dream." —C. S. LEWIS

INTENTION
Today I will have lots of creative energy.

PUMPKIN POWER

LOW-CALORIE • PROTEIN-PACKED

The bright orange color of this smoothie is a dead giveaway that pumpkin is loaded with beta-carotene. Pumpkin goes great in smoothies and should be a staple in any healthy diet. One serving of this skinny version of pumpkin pie has more than 200 percent of the daily value for vitamin A, is rich in antioxidants, and provides slow-burning carbohydrates.

Tip: *Freeze the pumpkin overnight to thicken the smoothie.*

1 cup unsweetened vanilla almond milk

½ cup silken tofu

½ cup canned pumpkin

½ cup frozen cranberries

1½ tablespoons hemp seed

1 graham cracker square, crushed

½ teaspoon vanilla extract

½ teaspoon pumpkin pie spice

1 cup ice

In a blender, combine all of the ingredients and blend until smooth. Serve right away.

VARIATION 1: Substitute cooked sweet potato or butternut squash for the pumpkin.

VARIATION 2: Add more graham crackers to boost the complex carbohydrates.

Nutritional info: calories: 292, fat: 13 grams, carbs: 30 grams, fiber: 8 grams, protein: 14 grams

SALAD PAIRING: BLACK BEAN MANGO SALAD, PAGE 148

"The harder the conflict, the more glorious the triumph." —THOMAS PAINE

INTENTION
Today I will be patient.

DANDELION GREEN

HIGH-FIBER • PROTEIN-PACKED

The high-fiber, low-calorie jicama adds a pear-like flavor to this smoothie made with green fruits and vegetables. Both cleansing and hydrating, this smoothie will leave you feeling fueled and energized.

Tip: Dandelion greens are high in calcium and loaded with vitamins, minerals, and antioxidants. Because they have a bitter taste, they are best paired with a sweet fruit like bananas to mask their flavor.

1 (11-ounce) container coconut water

1 (6-ounce) container vanilla soy yogurt

1 cup frozen spinach

1 cup fresh dandelion greens

½ cup jicama

¼ cup avocado

½ frozen banana

1 tablespoon lime juice

1 cup ice

In a blender, combine all of the ingredients and blend until smooth. Serve right away.

VARIATION 1: Substitute cucumber for the jicama.

VARIATION 2: Add 1 tablespoon of chia seeds for extra fiber and healthy omega-3 fats.

Nutritional info: calories: 417, fat: 9 grams, carbs: 76 grams, fiber: 15 grams, protein: 16 grams

SALAD PAIRING: RAW SLAW SALAD, PAGE 158

"When you reach the end of your rope, tie a knot and hang on." —FRANKLIN D. ROOSEVELT

INTENTION

Today I will notice the beauty.

RASPBERRY ALMOND

HEART-HEALTHY • HIGH-FIBER

This heart-healthy, high-fiber smoothie is made of antioxidant-rich raspberries, mango, and almond butter with a hint of cinnamon. High in healthy fats, fiber, vitamin C, potassium, and vitamin E, this rich-tasting smoothie meets half of your daily recommended intake of fiber.

Tip: One cup of raspberries has just 65 calories and a whopping 8 grams of dietary fiber.

1 cup unsweetened vanilla almond milk

1 tablespoon chia seeds

1 tablespoon almond butter

¾ cup frozen raspberries

½ cup frozen mango

½ teaspoon vanilla extract

½ teaspoon ground cinnamon

1 Medjool date, pitted

1 cup ice

In a blender, combine all of the ingredients and blend until smooth. Serve right away.

VARIATION 1: Substitute another nut butter for the almond butter or use 2 tablespoons of whole nuts.

VARIATION 2: Add 1 serving of protein powder.

Nutritional info: calories: 366, fat: 14 grams, carbs: 50 grams, fiber: 12 grams, protein: 8 grams

SALAD PAIRING: THE MIDDLE EASTERN SALAD, PAGE 155

"Always bear in mind that your resolution to succeed is more important than any one thing." —ABRAHAM LINCOLN

INTENTION
Today I will listen more.

BERRY BLUE TEA

LOW-CALORIE • BRAIN-BOOSTING

The antioxidant content of this sweet-tasting, low-calorie smoothie is off the charts! Goji berries, blueberries, and rooibos each contribute a unique phytochemical profile to this drink, making this a free radical–fighting superstar.

Tip: Brewed and cooled tea makes a great liquid base for smoothies. Rooibos, also known as African red tea, is high in antioxidants and is naturally caffeine-free.

1 cup brewed and cooled rooibos tea

½ cup silken tofu

1 cup frozen blueberries

2 tablespoons Goji berries, soaked in water for 15 minutes

1½ tablespoons hemp seeds

1 cup ice

In a blender, combine all of the ingredients and blend until smooth. Serve right away.

VARIATION 1: Substitute frozen raspberries for the Goji berries.

VARIATION 2: Add ¼ cup rolled oats.

Nutritional info: calories: 247, fat: 9 grams, carbs: 16 grams, fiber: 7 grams, protein: 11 grams

SALAD PAIRING: LENTIL BEET SALAD, PAGE 153

"Things do not happen, things are made to happen." —JOHN F. KENNEDY

INTENTION

Today I will try something new.

ORANGE CREAMSICLE

HEART-HEALTHY

This refreshing smoothie will start your day on a good note and keep your heart healthy with its cholesterol-lowering ingredients. Reminiscent of the indulgent frozen treat, this is one smoothie that your doctor will approve of.

Tip: Balance the sugar in fruit juices by having it with a portion of protein and healthy fats.

1 cup orange juice

1 (6-ounce) container vanilla soy yogurt

½ cup frozen mango

1 tablespoon ground flaxseed

½ teaspoon vanilla extract

2 tablespoons rolled oats

1 cup ice

In a blender, combine all of the ingredients and blend until smooth. Serve right away.

VARIATION 1: Substitute tofu for the soy yogurt.

VARIATION 2: Add 1 tablespoon raw cashews for thickness, as well as hearty-healthy monosaturated fats.

Nutritional info: calories: 380, fat: 6 grams, carbs: 74 grams, fiber: 5 grams, protein: 11 grams

SALAD PAIRING: HOPPIN' JOHN SALAD, PAGE 151

"Thinking is easy, acting is difficult, and to put one's thoughts into action is the most difficult thing in the world." —JOHANN WOLFGANG VON GOETHE

INTENTION
Today I will embrace my imperfections.

Congratulations on completing Week 2 of your 21-day healthy smoothie plan! After two weeks of following the suggested recipes, you should notice that your body craves its daily smoothie. You may also find that your cravings for processed foods and sugars have decreased and that your energy levels are steadier.

According to consumer research, the average American makes more than 200 food decisions each day (Wansink and Sobal, 2007)! Some of those decisions benefit your weight and health, while others don't. By getting into an eating routine and making it a habit to plan and prepare what you are going to eat each day, you can drastically reduce the number of not-so-great food decisions you make and tip the odds in your favor.

Coming up, you will have another week to try out some unique and energizing smoothies and nourishing salads. Continue to tune into your hunger and fullness cues as you go through your week; think through your food decisions; and take time to be active. As you head into Week 3, keep the words of French writer La Rochefoucauld in mind: "To eat is a necessity; to eat intelligently is an art."

NOTES

CHAPTER 7

WEEK 3

Congratulations on completing two weeks of your 21-day healthy smoothie plan! You have made it to Week 3 and should be noticing changes in the way you feel, your energy level, sleep patterns, and maybe even your weight. Coming up you will have seven more days to continue practicing your healthy new habits.

When developing and building new habits, it is common to experience challenges at this point. Busy schedules, travel, holidays, and unexpected problems are unavoidable and part of life. There is never a "best" or "right" time to begin a healthy eating routine or make changes. Instead, developing skills that will help you continue with your habits in the face of these challenges is what will make you successful in the long run.

To avoid falling off track, consider going to bed a bit earlier so you can get up in time to plan your day, prepare your smoothie and salad, and know when you are going to eat them. Awareness and a little organization facilitate making smart choices and sidestepping high-calorie processed foods and snacks. Consider finding an accountability partner to keep you on track with your healthy eating and fitness routines. Choose someone who shares similar goals and continue to strive for a little more and a little better each day this week.

MENU AT A GLANCE

	SMOOTHIE	SUGGESTED SALAD
MONDAY	Chocolate Mint *(page 126)*	Spinach Asparagus Salad *(page 159)*
TUESDAY	Pomegranate Beet Berry *(page 129)*	Spinach Avocado Sprout Salad *(page 159)*
WEDNESDAY	Blueberry Wheat Germ *(page 130)*	Broccoli Goji Bean Salad *(page 148)*
THURSDAY	Green Goddess *(page 133)*	Tofu, Tahini & Sweet Potato Salad *(page 162)*
FRIDAY	Pumpkin Seeds & Greens *(page 134)*	Cabbage Cucumber Hemp Seed Salad *(page 149)*
SATURDAY	Apple Pie *(page 137)*	Zucchini Walnut Salad *(page 162)*
SUNDAY	Cherry Chamomile Tea *(page 138)*	Kale Cashew Salad *(page 154)*

Before you start the week, set aside time on the weekend to do a full pantry review. Use the list in Chapter 4 (see page 67) to check your supplies and make a grocery list of items that you are running low on. At this point in the plan, you may be finding that you prefer several varieties of nuts, seeds, and fruits over others. Feel free to make substitutions based on your personal preferences, and customize the smoothies to suit your individual tastes. Do your shopping when you are not rushed and can take the time to get everything you need. A good way to stay on track with healthy eating is to schedule time each week to do menu planning, a pantry review, shopping, and prep. Set an alert on your phone for each of the activities so that you remember to do them. Being prepared will make it so much easier for you to stay on track with your healthy-eating plan.

The majority of the ingredients for the smoothies can simply be measured and tossed into the blender. However, to save time and make blending fast and convenient, allot time on Sunday to read through each recipe and prep and store the following ingredients:

Fresh produce: Chop ½ of a pear; measure out ¼ cup avocado; cook and slice 1 red beet, and portion out ¼ cup; slice 1 kiwi; slice and freeze ½ of a banana; grate ½ teaspoon fresh ginger; dice 1 medium green apple.

Liquids: Brew and cool 1 cup of chamomile tea and store it in the refrigerator.

Dairy: Measure out two ½-cup portions of silken tofu.

WEEK 3 SHOPPING LIST

SMOOTHIE SHOPPING LIST

To prepare the seven smoothies in Week 3 of your healthy smoothie plan, you will need the following ingredients:

Fresh produce
Vegetables: 1 beet
Fruit: 1 avocado, 1 pear, 1 kiwi, 1 banana, 1 green apple
Herbs: mint, ginger root

Frozen aisle
Vegetables: 2 cups spinach, 1 cup kale
Fruit: 1 cup strawberries, 1 cup blueberries, 1 cup cherries

Pantry
Seeds: 2 tablespoons hemp seeds, 2 tablespoons ground flaxseed, ¼ cup pumpkin seeds, 1 tablespoon chia seeds
Nuts: 2 tablespoons walnuts, 2 tablespoons raw cashews
Nut butter: ½ tablespoon peanut butter
Other: 1 tablespoon unsweetened cacao, ¼ cup wheat germ, ½ cup rolled oats, 1 Medjool date, 1 chamomile tea bag

Dairy
1 quart unsweetened vanilla almond milk (you will need 1½ cups)
1 (8-ounce) container 100-percent pomegranate juice
1 (15-ounce) package silken tofu
3 (6-ounce) containers vanilla soy yogurt
1 (11-ounce) container coconut water

Spices
Peppermint extract
Ground cinnamon

SUGGESTED SALADS SHOPPING LIST

There are seven suggested salads to go along with the smoothie recipes (see Chapter 8, pages 143 to 163, for recipes). The salads are simple and quick to prepare and include plant-based protein, healthy fats, and at least three or more servings of fruits and vegetables. Some of the same ingredients that are used in the smoothies are used in the salads in order to simplify your shopping and prep.

To prepare the suggested salads, you will need the following ingredients:

Fresh produce
Salad greens: 2 cups baby spinach, 2 cups kale, 2 cups mixed greens
Sprouts: 1 cup alfalfa sprouts, 1 cup pea shoots
Fresh vegetables: 2 cups broccoli, 1 red onion, 2 medium zucchini, 2 red bell peppers, 1 avocado, 1 cup shredded carrots, 1 medium sweet potato, ½ cup mushrooms, 1 cup shredded cabbage, 1 medium cucumber, ½ cup shelled edamame, 1 large tomato, 1 large stalk celery, 1 cup sugar snap peas, 10 grape tomatoes
Fresh herbs: basil, cilantro, dill, mint
Fresh fruit: 1 lemon

Pantry
Canned: 1 can cannellini beans, 1 jar artichoke hearts, 1 can hearts of palm, 1 can garbanzo beans
Dried fruit: 2 tablespoons Goji berries
Nuts: ¼ cup walnuts, ¼ cup sunflower seeds, ¼ cup raw cashews, 2 tablespoons slivered almonds
Nut butter: 1 tablespoon sesame tahini
Seeds: 1 tablespoon chia seeds, 2 tablespoons hemp seeds

Dairy
1 (15-ounce) package firm tofu

CHOCOLATE MINT

PROTEIN-PACKED • HIGH-FIBER • BRAIN-BOOSTING

This creamy decadent-tasting smoothie is packed with protein and healthy fats from the hemp seeds and avocado. It also has over half of your day's requirement for fiber and is loaded with calcium, iron, and vitamin C. The pear gives a hint of sweetness to the antioxidant-rich cacao, and the fresh mint brings together the flavors.

Tip: Mint is a natural stimulant, and the smell alone can be enough to charge your batteries when you are feeling sluggish. Mint also promotes digestion and soothes the stomach in cases of indigestion or inflammation.

1 cup unsweetened vanilla almond milk

2 tablespoons hemp seeds

1 cup frozen spinach

¼ cup avocado

½ pear

1 tablespoon unsweetened cacao

⅛ teaspoon peppermint extract

3 fresh mint leaves (optional)

1 cup ice

Add the almond milk to the blender, followed by the hemp seeds, and process into a thick paste. Add the remaining ingredients and blend until smooth. Serve right away.

VARIATION 1: Substitute yogurt or tofu for the almond milk.

VARIATION 2: Add 1 tablespoon cacao nibs to make it a mint–chocolate chip smoothie!

Nutritional info: calories: 372, fat: 22 grams, carbs: 28 grams, fiber: 15 grams, protein: 19 grams

SALAD PAIRING: SPINACH ASPARAGUS SALAD, PAGE 159

"Continuous effort—not strength or intelligence—is the key to unlocking potential." —WINSTON CHURCHILL

INTENTION
Today I will be a role model.

POMEGRANATE BEET BERRY

HEART-HEALTHY • BRAIN-BOOSTING

The use of pomegranate juice in this recipe allows you to reap the nutritional benefits this unique fruit has to offer without the difficulty of eating a fresh one. Pomegranates contain potent antioxidants, including polyphenols that have anti-cancer and immune-supporting effects. Combined with healthy fats and plant-based protein, this smoothie will nourish your immune system.

Tip: Beets are loaded with antioxidants, vitamin C, and folate, and have naturally occurring nitrates, which might increase exercise performance.

1 cup 100% pomegranate juice

½ cup silken tofu

¼ cup sliced cooked beets

1 cup frozen strawberries (or raspberries)

2 tablespoons chopped walnuts

1 cup ice

In a blender, combine all of the ingredients and blend until smooth. Serve right away.

VARIATION 1: Substitute nut butter for the walnuts.

VARIATION 2: Add 2 tablespoons ground flaxseed for additional fiber and omega-3 fats.

Nutritional info: calories: 325, fat: 11 grams, carbs: 50 grams, fiber: 4 grams, protein: 8 grams

SALAD PAIRING: SPINACH-AVOCADO-SPROUT SALAD, PAGE 159

"One cannot think well, love well, sleep well, if one has not dined well." —VIRGINIA WOOLF

INTENTION

Today I choose peace.

BLUEBERRY WHEAT GERM

HIGH-PROTEIN

Wheat germ kicks the nutrition of this smoothie up a notch by supplying B vitamins, vitamin E, fiber, minerals, protein, and healthy fats. Protein- and antioxidant-rich, this smoothie is great for breakfast or after a workout.

Tip: Wheat germ is the most vitamin- and mineral-rich part of the wheat kernel and is a source of phytosterols, which can lower bad cholesterol.

½ cup unsweetened vanilla almond milk

1 (6-ounce) container vanilla soy yogurt

¼ cup wheat germ

1 cup frozen blueberries

½ tablespoon peanut butter

1 cup ice

In a blender, combine all of the ingredients and blend until smooth. Serve right away.

VARIATION 1: Substitute tofu for the almond milk and add water as needed.

VARIATION 2: Add 1 cup of spinach to boost the vitamin A, K, and folate content.

Nutritional info: calories: 388, fat: 10 grams, carbs: 42 grams, fiber: 11 grams, protein: 16 grams

SALAD PAIRING: BROCCOLI GOJI BEAN SALAD, PAGE 148

"If the only tool you have is a hammer, you tend to see every problem as a nail." —ABRAHAM HAROLD MASLOW

INTENTION
Today I will try a different path.

GREEN GODDESS

BEAUTY-BOOSTING • HIGH-FIBER

This free radical–fighting smoothie will give you twice your daily recommended intake of vitamin C, omega-3 fats, and hydrating electrolytes. The kiwi gives this combination an invigorating taste reminiscent of strawberries and bananas.

Tip: Eating a couple of kiwifruit each day can lower your triglyceride levels and reduce your risk for blood clots.

1 (11-ounce) container coconut water

1 (6-ounce) container vanilla soy yogurt

1 cup frozen spinach

1 kiwi, peeled and sliced

2 tablespoons ground flaxseed

In a blender, combine all of the ingredients and blend until smooth. Serve right away.

VARIATION 1: Substitute almond milk for the coconut water for a creamier smoothie.

VARIATION 2: Add an additional kiwi to boost the fiber and vitamin C content.

Nutritional info: calories: 377, fat: 9 grams, carbs: 64 grams, fiber: 13 grams, protein: 16 grams

SALAD PAIRING: TOFU, TAHINI & SWEET POTATO SALAD, PAGE 162

"If we are peaceful, if we are happy, we can smile and blossom like a flower; and everyone in our family, our entire society, will benefit from our peace." —THICH NHAT HANH

INTENTION
Today I choose peace.

PUMPKIN SEEDS & GREENS

LOW-CALORIE

This spicy, green smoothie has ingredients that will hydrate and fuel you, leaving you feeling calm and nourished. Pumpkin seeds are rich in magnesium, one of the most critical minerals for helping your body cope with stress, along with healthy fats, fiber, and minerals. Drink up some cool refreshment and just breathe.

Tip: Sprouting seeds, like pumpkin, multiply the nutritional profile. The germination process also makes them easier to digest and increases their enzyme content.

1 cup unsweetened vanilla almond milk

1 cup frozen kale

½ frozen banana

¼ cup pumpkin seeds

½ teaspoon grated ginger

1 cup ice

In a blender, combine all of the ingredients and blend until smooth. Serve right away.

VARIATION 1: Substitute yogurt or tofu for the almond milk.

VARIATION 2: Add ½ of an avocado for extra creaminess and as a source of monounsaturated fats.

Nutritional info: calories: 260, fat: 15 grams, carbs: 23 grams, fiber: 5 grams, protein: 11 grams

SALAD PAIRING: CABBAGE CUCUMBER HEMP SEED SALAD, PAGE 149

"What you do speaks so loud, I cannot hear what you say." —RALPH WALDO EMERSON

INTENTION

Today I will be encouraging.

APPLE PIE

HEART-HEALTHY

A healthy version of a classic favorite, green apples and rolled oats make this smoothie high in cholesterol-lowering pectin and soluble fiber. The added cinnamon balances blood sugar while also giving the combination an apple pie flavor.

Tip: Mix the oats into the yogurt and let sit overnight in the refrigerator to add thickness to your smoothie.

1 (6-ounce) container vanilla soy yogurt

1 medium green apple, diced

½ cup rolled oats

1 Medjool date, pitted

½ teaspoon ground cinnamon

4 to 8 ounces water

1 cup ice

In a blender, combine all of the ingredients and blend until smooth. Serve right away.

VARIATION 1: Substitute almond milk for the yogurt and add ¼ cup avocado to keep the creamy consistency.

VARIATION 2: Add 1 tablespoon of chia seeds to make it extra thick and for added fiber and omega-3 fats.

Nutritional info: calories: 386, fat: 4 grams, carbs: 78 grams, fiber: 9 grams, protein: 8 grams

SALAD PAIRING: ZUCCHINI WALNUT SALAD, PAGE 162

"Step-by-step and the thing is done."
—CHARLES ATLAS

INTENTION
Today I will sit quietly for five minutes and clear my mind of negative thoughts.

CHERRY CHAMOMILE TEA

PROTEIN-PACKED

German chamomile has a long history of promoting restful sleep, but it makes a great smoothie base anytime of day. Coupled with antioxidant-rich cherries and healthy fats, this anti-inflammatory smoothie will soothe the nervous system and calm digestion.

Tip: Chamomile tea has a mild sedative effect and can ease anxiety.

1 cup brewed and cooled chamomile tea

½ cup silken tofu

1 cup frozen cherries

1 tablespoon chia seeds

2 tablespoons raw cashews

1 cup ice

In a blender, combine all of the ingredients and blend until smooth. Serve right away.

VARIATION 1: Substitute yogurt for the tofu.

VARIATION 2: Add ½ of a frozen banana for extra creaminess and some heart-healthy potassium.

Nutritional info: calories: 372, fat: 19 grams, carbs: 39 grams, fiber: 8 grams, protein: 13 grams

SALAD PAIRING: KALE CASHEW SALAD, PAGE 154

"One of the greatest discoveries a man makes, one of his great surprises is to find he can do what he was afraid he couldn't do." —HENRY FORD

INTENTION
Today I will replenish my spirit.

WEEKLY WRAP-UP

WEEK 3

Congratulations on completing your 3-day detox cleanse and 21-day healthy smoothie plan! Healthy eating is not about deprivation or strict dietary limitations; instead, it embraces feeling great, having more energy, and stabilizing your mood. Now that you have completed the plan, you are encouraged to continue with your habit of replacing one meal a day with a healthy smoothie.

Here are some tips to help you maintain your new habits:

- Set yourself up for success! Continue to reserve time each week to prepare a menu, perform a pantry review, go shopping, and do weekly food prep.
- Eat from the rainbow. Think of your diet in terms of color, variety, and freshness. Keep processed foods to a minimum.
- Every change you make to your diet matters. Celebrate each success that you have no matter how small.
- Expect the unexpected. There will always be challenges that can get in the way of your healthy eating routine. Lose the all-or-none thinking and don't let one slip-up derail all of your new habits.
- Be mindful of how you eat. Slow down, chew, eat slowly, and tune into hunger and fullness cues. Listen to your body.
- Be active each day. Find an activity that you enjoy and aim for doing it 30 minutes daily.
- By planning a healthy diet as a number of small, manageable steps and approaching the changes with commitment, you will be able to maintain a healthy lifestyle in no time.

NOTES

CHAPTER 8

STELLAR SALADS

For days when you want to expand your stellar eating habits beyond the blender, these tasty, filling, nutritionally complete salads will make excellent complements to your smoothie meal. Most importantly, they're super easy to throw together—no cooking required! Enjoy these meal-sized salads on the same day as their suggested smoothie pairings, or any time you need a quick, delicious dish.

APPLE-WHEAT GERM SALAD

Wheat germ adds a nutritious crunch to this antioxidant-rich salad. Wheat germ is high in protein, vitamin E, folic acid, and zinc. Combined with healthy fats from nuts and antioxidants and cholesterol-lowering fiber from the apple, this superfood combination will keep you fueled and energized.

1 cup fresh green beans, trimmed and steamed

1 medium apple, cored and diced

1 cup sliced red bell pepper

2 tablespoons chopped walnuts

2 tablespoons wheat germ

2 tablespoons slivered almonds

1 tablespoon orange zest

2 tablespoons chopped fresh parsley

2 cups baby spinach

In a large bowl, combine all of the ingredients except the spinach and mix. Pour mixture over the fresh spinach. Dress with dressing of your choice. Serve immediately.

Nutritional info: calories: 368, fat: 19 grams, carbs: 42 grams, fiber: 12 grams, protein: 14 grams

ARTICHOKE BEAN SALAD

Hearts of palm and artichoke hearts make this salad high in iron, fiber, and calcium. Protein-rich garbanzo beans and slivered almonds supply long-lasting energy. Toss a handful of blueberries or raspberries on top in place of dressing for an antioxidant-rich boost.

2 cups mixed salad greens

½ cup canned garbanzo beans, drained and rinsed

10 grape tomatoes

4 artichoke hearts, drained and quartered

4 hearts of palm, drained and chopped into bite-sized pieces

2 tablespoons slivered almonds

On a medium plate, place the salad greens. Arrange the beans, tomatoes, artichoke hearts, and hearts of palm on the greens. Top with the slivered almonds. Dress the salad with a dressing of your choice. Serve immediately.

Nutritional info: calories: 296, fat: 10 grams, carbs: 38 grams, fiber: 9 grams, protein: 18 grams

AVOCADO CELERY SALAD

Adding ½ of an avocado to your lunch may keep you more satisfied and reduce your cravings. Avocados are low in carbohydrates and provide about 8 percent of the daily value for fiber. They are also an excellent source of vitamin C and monounsaturated fats. Paired with the healthy blood pressure promoting effects of celery and sesame seeds, this is one heart-healthy and waistline-friendly meal.

½ cup canned red beans, drained and rinsed

½ cup halved grape tomatoes

½ cup sliced celery

½ medium avocado, cubed

1 medium lime, juiced

1 tablespoon chopped fresh cilantro

1 medium green onion, sliced

1 tablespoon black or white sesame seeds

In a large bowl, add the beans, tomatoes, celery, avocado, lime, and cilantro. Toss to combine. Top with green onion and sesame seeds. Serve and enjoy.

Nutritional info: calories: 344, fat: 17 grams, carbs: 41 grams, fiber: 17 grams, protein: 12 grams

BERRY BEET JICAMA SALAD

Beets and berries combine for a salad rich in phytochemicals, anti-cancer properties, and blood pressure–lowering factors. Jicama adds a crunchy, sweet taste to this salad, but if you can't find it, substitute fresh fennel. And don't throw out your beet greens! Use them in place of kale in recipes.

1 medium beet, cooked and sliced

½ cup sliced jicama

½ cup blueberries or sliced strawberries

¼ cup thinly sliced sweet white onion

¼ cup walnuts

½ tablespoon balsamic vinegar

½ tablespoon orange juice

1 teaspoon olive oil

2 cups mixed greens

In a medium bowl, combine the beet, jicama, berries, onion, and walnuts. In a small bowl, whisk together vinegar, orange juice, and olive oil. Add to beet mixture and toss gently. Chill before serving on top of mixed salad greens.

Nutritional info: calories: 348, fat: 23 grams, carbs: 34 grams, fiber: 9 grams, protein: 8 grams

BLACK BEAN AND TOFU SALAD

This high-protein salad takes on a Mexican flare with the combination of avocado, green pepper, and fresh cilantro. All beans are high in protein and fiber, but what makes this bean unique is the color coat, which contains more than eight different flavonoids that act as antioxidants. Enjoy this salad with some fresh pico de gallo.

2 cups mixed salad greens

½ cup black beans, drained and rinsed

½ cup crumbled tofu

½ cup diced green bell pepper

½ medium avocado, sliced

4 grape tomatoes

Fresh cilantro

In a large bowl, place salad greens. If using canned beans, rinse with cold water in a colander to remove excess sodium and add to the greens. Arrange the remaining ingredients on top of the greens. Dress the salad with dressing of your choice. Serve immediately.

Nutritional info: calories: 356, fat: 17 grams, carbs: 38 grams, fiber: 15 grams, protein: 22 grams

KALE CUCUMBER SALAD

Detoxify and hydrate with this salad made of antioxidant-rich kale and cucumbers. Both vegetables provide support for the digestive system and are anti-inflammatories. Toss some mint leaves on top to boost the digestive power of this salad. (PICTURED AT RIGHT)

2 cups curly kale

Olive oil for rubbing kale

1 cup steamed fresh green beans

1 medium cucumber, sliced

4 grape tomatoes

½ cup chopped carrots

½ cup crumbled firm tofu

Wash kale and dry off excess water by blotting on a paper towel. Coat hands with olive oil and rub kale until it is softened and bright green. Arrange ingredients on the kale and top with crumbled firm tofu. Dress the salad with the dressing of your choice. Serve immediately.

Nutritional info: calories: 312, fat: 9 grams, carbs: 42 grams, fiber: 10 grams, protein: 23 grams

BLACK BEAN MANGO SALAD

Crispy low-calorie jicama compliments this high-protein, nutrient-rich salad made of black beans and mangos. High in vitamin C, fiber, and monounsaturated fats, the sweet and savory combination will please your taste buds.

2 cups mixed salad greens

½ cup canned black beans, drained and rinsed

½ fresh mango, sliced

½ avocado, sliced

½ cup sliced jicama

1 tomato, sliced

¼ cup crumbled firm tofu (or cheddar-flavor soy cheese)

Fresh cilantro

In a large bowl, place salad greens. If using canned beans, rinse with cold water in a colander to remove excess sodium and add to the greens. Arrange the remaining ingredients on top of the greens. Dress the salad with dressing of your choice. Serve immediately.

Nutritional info: calories: 350, fat: 13 grams, carbs: 47 grams, fiber: 15 grams, protein: 15 grams

BROCCOLI GOJI BEAN SALAD

Tantalize your taste buds with this crunchy, chewy, nutrient-rich salad. Cannellini beans supply blood sugar–balancing fiber and protein to keep you fueled and satisfied. Chia seeds provide an omega-3-filled crunch, Goji berries add an antioxidant-rich chew, and broccoli contributes an antioxidant-rich crunch.

2 tablespoons Goji berries, soaked in water for 15 minutes

2 cups chopped broccoli

½ cup chopped red onion

½ cup canned cannellini beans, drained and rinsed

1 tablespoon chia seeds

In a large bowl, mix all of the ingredients. Dress the salad with dressing of your choice. Serve immediately.

Nutritional info: calories: 287, fat: 4 grams, carbs: 50 grams, fiber: 17 grams, protein: 13 grams

BRUSSELS SPROUTS AND CAULIFLOWER SALAD

Cruciferous vegetables blend together in this detoxifying antioxidant-rich salad. Cauliflower and Brussels sprouts are rich in phytonutrients that provide digestive support, decrease inflammation, and support heart health. High in vitamins C, K, and folate, you will want to include these vegetable powerhouses in your diet on a regular basis.

1 cup steamed halved Brussels sprouts

1 cup steamed chopped cauliflower

1 cup sliced mushrooms

4 sun-dried tomatoes packed in oil, sliced

¼ cup slivered almonds

In a large bowl, place all of the ingredients and toss until coated with the oil from the tomatoes. Serve immediately.

Nutritional info: calories: 275, fat: 17 grams, carbs: 22 grams, fiber: 10 grams, protein: 14 grams

CABBAGE CUCUMBER HEMP SEED SALAD

This protein-rich salad is high in cholesterol-lowering nutrients, omega-3 fats, and vitamins A and C. Cabbage has a type of fiber that binds to cholesterol, promoting healthier levels. It also boasts an array of phytochemicals and anti-inflammatory nutrients.

1 cup shredded cabbage

½ cup shredded carrots

1 medium cucumber, sliced

½ cup shelled edamame

2 tablespoons hemp seeds

On a medium plate, layer the cabbage, carrots, cucumber slices, and edamame. Sprinkle with the hemp seeds. Dress the salad with dressing of your choice. Serve immediately.

Nutritional info: calories: 373, fat: 17 grams, carbs: 36 grams, fiber: 9 grams, protein: 22 grams

CANNELLINI BEAN SALAD

Cannellini beans, also known as white kidney beans, lead the pack with their low-glycemic score and their ability to provide steady and slow-burning energy. The added fiber from the artichoke hearts makes this nutritious combination a filling meal that will stave off cravings.

2 cups mixed salad greens

½ cup canned cannellini beans, drained and rinsed

1 cup steamed fresh green beans

½ cup sliced red bell peppers

4 artichoke hearts, quartered

2 sliced sun-dried tomatoes, packed in oil

In a large bowl, place salad greens. If using canned beans, rinse with cold water in a colander to remove excess sodium. Arrange the remaining ingredients on top of the greens. Dress the salad with dressing of your choice. Serve immediately.

Nutritional info: calories: 223, fat: 0.2 grams, carbs: 42 grams, fiber: 11 grams, protein: 15 grams

EDAMAME SALAD

Edamame is just a fancy name for boiled soybeans, but the secret is they are delicious and a star legume! Just ½ cup of shelled edamame has 120 calories, 9 grams of fiber, and 11 grams of complete protein, meaning it has all of the essential amino acids that your body needs.

2 cups mixed salad greens

1 cup steamed sugar snap peas

1 cup steamed and shelled edamame

1 cup thinly shredded cabbage

½ cup shredded carrots

1 teaspoon grated ginger

In a large bowl, place salad greens. Arrange the remaining ingredients on top of the greens. Dress the salad with dressing of your choice. Serve immediately.

Nutritional info: calories: 206, fat: 4 grams, carbs: 30 grams, fiber: 9 grams, protein: 15 grams

GREEN PEA EDAMAME SALAD

This protein-rich salad combines high-quality soy protein with plant-powered omega-3 fats and phytochemical-rich cruciferous vegetables. A sweet and crunchy mix, this salad is blood sugar–balancing and can decrease one's risk for chronic disease.

1 cup kale, sliced thin

½ cup chopped broccoli

½ cup fresh or thawed frozen green peas

½ cup shelled edamame

½ cup shredded carrots

1 tablespoon hemp seeds

1 teaspoon olive oil

In a large bowl, place all of the ingredients and mix until combined. Serve immediately.

Nutritional info: calories: 373, fat: 14 grams, carbs: 44 grams, fiber: 13 grams, protein: 23 grams

HOPPIN' JOHN SALAD

A symbol of good luck in Southern New Year's Day dishes, it would be a shame to limit its consumption to holidays. Black-eyed peas are a high-fiber, low–glycemic index legume, and are especially good at keeping your blood sugar balanced after you eat them.

2 cups mixed salad greens

½ cup cooked black-eyed peas

1 cup steamed sugar snap peas

½ cup chopped green bell pepper

½ cup chopped onion

4 grape tomatoes

Dash cumin

Dash paprika

In a large bowl, place salad greens. If using canned black-eyed peas, rinse with cold water in a colander to remove excess sodium and add to the greens. Arrange the remaining ingredients on top of the greens. Dress the salad with dressing of your choice. Serve immediately.

Nutritional info: calories: 223, fat: 1 gram, carbs: 41 grams, fiber: 9 grams, protein: 15 grams

LENTIL BEET SALAD

Blood sugar–balancing lentils boost the protein content of this antioxidant-rich salad. Rich in folate, potassium, fiber, and vitamin C, the beets, lentils, and orange juice are an excellent combination for promoting heart health. Fennel provides a unique volatile oil that has been shown to reduce inflammation and the risk for certain types of cancer. (PICTURED AT LEFT)

2 cups mixed salad greens

1 cup cooked lentils

1 medium beet, cooked and sliced

1 cup sliced mushrooms

1 small bulb fresh fennel, thinly sliced

1 tablespoon orange juice

In a large bowl, place salad greens and top with the lentils, beets, mushrooms, and fennel. Drizzle with orange juice. Dress the salad with dressing of your choice. Serve immediately.

Nutritional info: calories: 295, fat: 0.7 grams, carbs: 29 grams, fiber: 19 grams, protein: 22 grams

KALE BROCCOLI SLAW SALAD

Enjoy this salad as a main dish or as a filling for a wrap or sandwich. Kale is an excellent source of vitamins A, C, and K and manganese, and a very good source of fiber, calcium, vitamin B_6, potassium, and iron.

2 cups finely sliced kale

1 broccoli stem, peeled, finely sliced or grated

1 small carrot, finely sliced or grated

1 small zucchini, finely sliced or grated

⅔ cup green peas, fresh or thawed frozen

½ apple or pear, grated

½ tablespoon hemp seeds

½ tablespoon olive oil

1 tablespoon cider vinegar

½ teaspoon Dijon mustard

1 teaspoon honey

In a large mixing bowl, combine kale, broccoli, carrot, zucchini, peas, and apple. Toss lightly to mix. In a separate bowl, whisk together the rest of the ingredients until combined. Pour the dressing over the salad, toss to coat, and allow to marinate for at least a few hours in the refrigerator. Serve chilled.

Nutritional info: calories: 372, fat: 11 grams, carbs: 59 grams, fiber: 14 grams, protein: 16 grams

KALE CASHEW SALAD

This nutritious salad is high in vitamins and minerals, including vitamins A, C, and K. Celery provides a crunch and blood pressure–lowering factors, while the cashews add plant-based protein and heart-healthy fats. Mint is added to promote digestion.

Olive oil for rubbing kale

2 cups kale

1 large tomato, sliced

1 large celery stalk, sliced

1 cup steamed sugar snap peas

¼ cup raw cashews

1 tablespoon fresh mint

Coat hands with olive oil and rub kale until it is softened and bright green. Arrange tomato, celery, and sugar snap peas on top of the kale. Sprinkle with cashews and garnish with fresh mint. Dress the salad with dressing of your choice. Serve immediately.

Nutritional info: calories: 302, fat: 15 grams, carbs: 29 grams, fiber: 5 grams, protein: 11 grams

LENTIL CAULIFLOWER SALAD

Lentils, part of the legume family, are small but nutritionally mighty. Lentils are an excellent source of fiber, vitamins, minerals, and proteins. The type of fiber in lentils can lower cholesterol and steady blood sugar levels. Lentils make a delicious addition to salads, soups, and whole grains.

2 cups salad greens

2 cups steamed cauliflower

1 cup cooked lentils

4 button mushrooms

1 tablespoon sunflower seeds

In a large bowl, place salad greens. Arrange the remaining ingredients on top of the greens. Dress the salad with dressing of your choice. Serve immediately.

Nutritional info: calories: 362, fat: 4 grams, carbs: 14 grams, fiber: 20 grams, protein: 25 grams

LIMA BEAN AND FLAXSEED SALAD

This salad uses frozen beans and broccoli and lets them thaw instead of cooking them to cut down on prep time. Lima beans, also known as butter beans, are a very good source of cholesterol-lowering fiber, which also prevents blood sugar from rising too rapidly after meals. With a topping of ground flaxseed, this easy-to-prepare salad works great as a lunch or as a topping for cooked grains.

½ cup frozen green beans

½ cup frozen lima beans

1 cup frozen broccoli

¼ cup chopped red bell pepper

¼ cup chopped onion

1 teaspoon olive oil

2 teaspoons apple cider vinegar

Ground black pepper

2 tablespoons ground flaxseed

In a large bowl with a tight-fitting lid, combine green beans, lima beans, broccoli, bell pepper, and onion. In a small bowl, mix together the olive oil, vinegar, and black pepper. Pour olive oil mixture over bean mixture. Seal lid and shake bowl until mixture is evenly coated. Refrigerate for 24 hours or until ingredients are completely thawed. Shake well and top with ground flaxseed before serving.

Nutritional info: calories: 305, fat: 10 grams, carbs: 36 grams, fiber: 12 grams, protein: 12 grams

THE MIDDLE EASTERN SALAD

Hummus, a spread made from chickpeas, sesame tahini, lemon juice, and olive oil, could help you with weight management while lowering your cholesterol. Rich in protein, hummus can help fight cravings and balance blood sugar. The iron content in hummus helps boost energy, which could make you more motivated to hit the gym.

2 cups mixed salad greens

1 cup steamed fresh greens beans

1 large tomato, sliced

¼ cup prepared hummus

1 sprig fresh mint

1 whole-grain pita bread cut into triangles

In a large bowl, place salad greens. Arrange the remaining ingredients on top of the greens. Dress the salad with dressing of your choice. Serve immediately.

Nutritional info: calories: 365, fat: 11 grams, carbs: 56 grams, fiber: 11 grams, protein: 14 grams

POWER SALAD

Salads don't have to be complicated to be full of nutrition. This salad is high in vitamins A, C, and folate and provides one-third of your daily recommended intake of fiber. It is loaded with antioxidants and has as much protein as 2½ eggs, yet it's all plant based.

2 cups mixed salad greens

3 to 4 baby broccoli stalks, steamed

½ cup pea shoots

½ cup alfalfa sprouts

1 tablespoon pumpkin seeds

½ cup garbanzo beans, drained and rinsed

6 grape tomatoes

In a large bowl, place salad greens. Arrange the remaining ingredients on top of the greens. Dress the salad with dressing of your choice. Serve immediately.

Nutritional info: calories: 246, fat: 8 grams, carbs: 32 grams, fiber: 8 grams, protein: 18 grams

PAPAYA LENTIL SALAD

Papayas are one of those neglected fruits that deserve a second look. Eating papaya, which is high in vitamin C, B vitamins, minerals, and antioxidants, may support immune health, protect against heart disease, and promote digestive health. Lentils provide slow-burning, long-lasting energy and plant-based protein.
(PICTURED AT RIGHT)

1 cup cooked lentils, drained and rinsed

1 plum tomato, chopped

½ cup sliced papaya

1 tablespoon fresh lemon juice

1 teaspoon olive oil

1 green onion, finely sliced

1 tablespoon fresh parsley

1 tablespoon Goji berries, soaked for 15 minutes

In a large mixing bowl, add the lentils, tomato, papaya, lemon juice, and olive oil. Toss to combine. Top with green onion, parsley, and Goji berries. Serve immediately.

Nutritional info: calories: 339, fat: 5 grams, carbs: 34 grams, fiber: 19 grams, protein: 20 grams

RAW SLAW SALAD

Quick and easy to prepare, this simple slaw is high in vitamin C, fiber, and complete high-quality protein. Grate some ginger on top for added digestive enzymes and a spicy kick.

2 cups shredded cabbage

½ cup sliced red bell pepper

1 cup shredded carrots

½ cup shelled edamame

2 tablespoons peanuts

1 cup pea shoots

In a large bowl, place cabbage. Arrange the remaining ingredients on top of the cabbage. Dress the salad with dressing of your choice. Serve immediately.

Nutritional info: calories: 338, fat: 11 grams, carbs: 46 grams, fiber: 16 grams, protein: 18 grams

THE SIMPLE VEGAN SALAD

One serving of this salad will give you more than seven servings of vegetables! Nutritionally balanced with healthy fats from pumpkin seeds and complete high-quality soy protein from tofu, this meal will satisfy your hunger for hours.

2 cups mixed salad greens

1 cup steamed broccoli

1 serving sliced baked tofu

1 cup shredded carrots

1 cup alfalfa sprouts

1 tablespoon pumpkin seeds

4 grape tomatoes

In a large bowl, place salad greens. Arrange the remaining ingredients on top of the greens. Dress the salad with dressing of your choice. Serve immediately.

Nutritional info: calories: 349, fat: 14 grams, carbs: 32 grams, fiber: 12 grams, protein: 28 grams

SPINACH ASPARAGUS SALAD

This filling salad highlights asparagus, which contains a type of probiotic fiber known as inulin. Inulin feeds the good bacteria in your large intestine and can increase your nutrient absorption, lower your risk of allergy, and lower your risk of colon cancer.

2 cups baby spinach

2 cups asparagus spears, rinsed, ends trimmed, and cut into 1-inch pieces

½ pear, sliced

¼ cup raw cashews

½ cup organic pea shoots

½ cup sliced red bell pepper

In a large bowl, place spinach. Arrange ingredients on top of the spinach. Dress the salad with the dressing of your choice. Serve immediately.

Nutritional info: calories: 370, fat: 13 grams, carbs: 51 grams, fiber: 15 grams, protein: 20 grams

SPINACH AVOCADO SPROUT SALAD

The nutrients in this salad are off the charts due to the use of alfalfa sprouts and pea shoots. Harvested before they become full-grown plants, sprouts and shoots contain concentrated amounts of nutrients and are very low in calories. Remember to rinse your sprouts before adding to your salad to reduce your risk of foodborne illness.

2 cups baby spinach

½ avocado, sliced

½ cup chopped red bell pepper

1 cup alfalfa sprouts

1 cup pea shoots

½ cup shredded carrots

¼ cup sunflower seeds

Fresh cilantro for garnish

On a medium plate, arrange the baby spinach. Arrange the avocado, bell pepper, alfalfa sprouts, pea shoots, and shredded carrots on top of the spinach. Sprinkle with sunflower seeds and garnish with fresh cilantro. Dress the salad with dressing of your choice. Serve immediately.

Nutritional info: calories: 397, fat: 30 grams, carbs: 26 grams, fiber: 13 grams, protein: 15 grams

SALAD IN A JAR

Packing your lunch for work can seem like a chore and a difficult practice to sustain, but it doesn't have to be that way. A mason jar salad is a portable, healthy, easy-to-make lunch and offers plenty of room for variety. It also solves the problem of a soggy salad or bringing a separate dressing container.
(PICTURED AT LEFT)

½ cup chopped broccoli

½ cup chopped tomato

½ cup black beans, drained and rinsed

1 tablespoon pumpkin seeds

1 tablespoon olive oil

2 cups salad greens

To prepare a mason jar salad, you just need to keep a few things in mind: Pour the salad dressing into the bottom of the jar and begin to layer (from the bottom up) the heartiest ingredients first to the most tender ingredients last. Finish by topping the salad with salad greens, making sure that they are tightly packed. Seal with a lid and store in the fridge for up to a week.

Nutritional info: calories: 363, fat: 19 grams, carbs: 36 grams, fiber: 13 grams, protein: 16 grams

A TASTE OF ITALY SALAD

Black olives, basil, asparagus, and artichoke hearts are a powerful combination for promoting heart health in this tasty Italian-inspired salad. Rich in monounsaturated fats and soluble fiber, the addition of basil boosts the blood vessel protective qualities of this vegetable mix.

2 large tomatoes, sliced into rounds

6 large asparagus stalks, trimmed and steamed

4 artichoke hearts, quartered

6 medium black olives

½ cup crumbled firm tofu (or mozzarella-flavor soy cheese)

Fresh basil for garnish

On a medium plate, cover with the tomato slices. Place the remaining ingredients on top of the tomatoes. Dress the salad with dressing of your choice. Serve immediately.

Nutritional info: calories: 195, fat: 6 grams, carbs: 12 grams, fiber: 4 grams, protein: 12 grams

TOFU, TAHINI & SWEET POTATO SALAD

A cooked sweet potato serves as the base for this hearty salad. Loaded in beta-carotene, vitamin C, fiber, and healthy fats from sesame tahini, this is one salad that will keep you fueled and satisfied.

½ **cup crumbled firm tofu**

1 **tablespoon sesame tahini**

1 **teaspoon lemon juice**

2 **tablespoons chopped fresh dill**

Pinch salt

Freshly ground black pepper

1 **medium sweet potato, cooked and sliced into wedges**

½ **cup chopped red bell pepper**

½ **cup sliced mushrooms**

In a small bowl, combine tofu, sesame tahini, lemon juice, dill, salt, and black pepper, and mash until all of the ingredients are combined. Top the potato with the tofu mixture and add the bell pepper and mushrooms. Serve immediately.

Nutritional info: calories: 362, fat: 15 grams, carbs: 44 grams, fiber: 12 grams, protein: 17 grams

ZUCCHINI WALNUT SALAD

Mix things up with this salad using thinly sliced zucchini as the base. Zucchini is very low in calories and is a good source of vitamins, minerals, and fiber. The low-calorie content of zucchini pairs well with a serving of heart-healthy walnuts and plant-based protein.

2 **medium zucchini, sliced paper thin**

1 **red bell pepper, sliced in rounds**

½ **cup crumbled firm tofu**

¼ **cup chopped walnuts**

1 **tablespoon fresh basil**

On a medium plate, layer the zucchini slices. Arrange the bell pepper on top of the zucchini. Crumble the tofu on top of the vegetables. Top with walnuts and fresh basil. Dress the salad with dressing of your choice. Serve immediately.

Nutritional info: calories: 390, fat: 26 grams, carbs: 25 grams, fiber: 8 grams, protein: 21 grams

APPENDIX A
THE DIRTY DOZEN AND THE CLEAN FIFTEEN

The **Dirty Dozen** are foods that have high levels of pesticide residues when conventionally grown. In 2014, the Environmental Working Group recommended buying the organic versions of the following whenever possible:

- Apples
- Celery
- Cherry tomatoes
- Cucumbers
- Grapes
- Nectarines
- Peaches
- Potatoes
- Snap peas
- Spinach
- Strawberries
- Sweet bell peppers

The **Clean Fifteen** were found to have the lowest amounts of pesticide contamination in 2014, and are considered safe to buy conventionally grown (nonorganic):

- Asparagus
- Avocados
- Cabbage
- Cantaloupe (domestic)
- Cauliflower
- Eggplants
- Grapefruits
- Kiwis
- Mangos
- Onions
- Papayas
- Pineapples
- Sweet corn
- Sweet peas (frozen)
- Sweet potatoes

BLENDERS

BRAND	TYPE	PRICE	VOLUME
Blendtec Designer 625 with Wildside+ Jar	High-speed	$479.99	96 qt
Hamilton Beech HBH650 3 HP Tempest	High-speed	$459.00	64 oz.
Vitamix 5200 Standard	High-speed	$449.00	64 oz.
Vitamix Personal Blender	High-speed	$409.00	20 & 40 oz.
Blendtec Classic 575	High-speed	$379.99	64 oz.
Nutri Ninja – Ninja Blender Duo with Auto-IQ	High-speed	Starting at $199.00	18, 24, & 32 oz.
Cuisinart Power Edge 700 Blender	High-speed	$149.99	56 oz.
Oster Performance Blender with Food Processor and Blend'N go cups	High-speed	$149.99	64 oz.
Oster BCCG08-RFP-NP9	High-speed	$51.99	48 oz.
Magic Bullet MBR-1701	High-speed	$38.82	Tall, short cups
Magic Bullet NutriBullet NBR-12 12-Piece High-Speed Blender/Mixer System	High-speed	$89.00	Tall, short cups
Cuisinart SmartStick Hand Blender	Immersion	$34.95	n/a
Hamilton Beech 58148 Power Elite Multi-function blender	Standard	$26.99	40 oz.
Hamilton Beech Single Serve	Low-powered	$19.99	14 oz.

Prices vary by retailer.

BRAND	SETTINGS	POWER	BEST FOR
Blendtec Designer 625 with Wildside+ Jar	Preprogrammed cycles, 6 speeds	3 peak HP	Smoothies, ice cream, whole juices, hot soups
Hamilton Beech HBH650 3 HP Tempest	2 speeds plus pulse	3 peak HP	Smoothies, ice cream, salsa, hot soups
Vitamix 5200 Standard	High/low, 10 settings	2 peak HP	Smoothies, hot soups, frozen desserts
Vitamix Personal Blender	Variable, 10 settings	790 watts	Smoothies
Blendtec Classic 575	Preprogrammed cycles, 5 speeds	3 peak HP	Smoothies, salsa, hot soups
Nutri Ninja – Ninja Blender Duo with Auto-IQ	5 programs, 3 speeds	1,500 watts	Smoothies, salsa, hot soups
Cuisinart Power Edge 700 Blender	Preprogrammed	700 watts	Smoothies, hot soups, sauces
Oster Performance Blender with Food Processor and Blend'N go cups	Preprogrammed and manual	1,100 watts	Smoothies, whole juices, shakes
Oster BCCG08-RFP-NP9	8 speeds	450 watts	Smoothies, salsa, hot soups
Magic Bullet MBR-1701	1 speed	250 watts	Smoothies
Magic Bullet NutriBullet NBR-12 12-Piece High-Speed Blender/Mixer System	1 speed	600 watts	Smoothies, green juices, hot soups
Cuisinart SmartStick Hand Blender	2 speeds	200 watts	Cold drinks, hot soups
Hamilton Beech 58148 Power Elite Multi-function blender	12 speeds	700 watts	Smoothies, salsa, purees
Hamilton Beech Single Serve	1 speed	175 watts	Smoothies, baby food, salad dressings

MEASUREMENT CONVERSION CHARTS

VOLUME EQUIVALENTS (LIQUID)

U.S. STANDARD	U.S. STANDARD (OUNCES)	METRIC (APPROXIMATE)
2 tablespoons	1 fl. oz.	30 mL
¼ cup	2 fl. oz.	60 mL
½ cup	4 fl. oz.	120 mL
1 cup	8 fl. oz.	240 mL
1½ cups	12 fl. oz.	355 mL
2 cups or 1 pint	16 fl. oz.	475 mL
4 cups or 1 quart	32 fl. oz.	1 L
1 gallon	128 fl. oz.	4 L

VOLUME EQUIVALENTS (DRY)

U.S. STANDARD	METRIC (APPROXIMATE)
⅛ teaspoon	0.5 mL
¼ teaspoon	1 mL
½ teaspoon	2 mL
¾ teaspoon	4 mL
1 teaspoon	5 mL
1 tablespoon	15 mL
¼ cup	59 mL
⅓ cup	79 mL
½ cup	118 mL
⅔ cup	156 mL
¾ cup	177 mL
1 cup	235 mL
2 cups or 1 pint	475 mL
3 cups	700 mL
4 cups or 1 quart	1 L
½ gallon	2 L
1 gallon	4 L

OVEN TEMPERATURES

FAHRENHEIT (F)	CELSIUS (C) (APPROXIMATE)
250	120
300	150
325	165
350	180
375	190
400	200
425	220
450	230

WEIGHT EQUIVALENTS

U.S. STANDARD	METRIC (APPROXIMATE)
½ ounce	15 g
1 ounce	30 g
2 ounces	60 g
4 ounces	115 g
8 ounces	225 g
12 ounces	340 g
16 ounces or 1 pound	455 g

REFERENCES

Amazon.com. "Best Blenders." Accessed November 4, 2014. http://www.amazon.com
/s/ref=nb_sb_noss_2?url=search-alias%3Daps&field-keywords=best%20blenders.

Amazon.com. "Ball Freezer Jars." Accessed November 4, 2014. http://www.amazon.com
/s/ref=nb_sb_noss?url=search-alias%3Daps&field-keywords=ball+freezer+jars&rh
=i%3Aaps%2Ck%3Aball+freezer+jars.

Blendtec. Accessed November 4, 2014. http://www.blendtec.com/blenders?gclid=CK7
WhYW38MECFU1hfgodbUIABQ.

Duhigg, Charles. *The Power of Habit: Why We Do What We Do in Life and Business.* New
York: Random House, 2012.

EcoJarz. Accessed November 4, 2014. http://www.ecojarz.com.

Healthy Smoothie Headquarters. Accessed October 30, 2014. http://www
.healthysmoothiehq.com.

Johns Hopkins Medicine. "Caffeine Withdrawal Recognized as a Disorder." Accessed
October 21, 2014. http://www.hopkinsmedicine.org/press_releases/2004
/09_29_04.html.

Leenders, Max, Sluijs, Ivonne, Ros, Martine, Boshuizen, Hendriek, Siersema, Peter,
Ferrari, Pietro, Weikert, Cornelia, et al., "Fruit and Vegetable Consumption and
Mortality: European Prospective Investigation into Cancer and Nutrition." *American
Journal of Epidemiology* 178, no. 4 (2013): 590–602. Doi: 10.1093/aje/kwt006.
Accessed November 1, 2014. http://aje.oxfordjournals.org/content/178/4/590.

Mayo Clinic. "Sleep." Accessed October 29, 2014. http://www.mayoclinic.org/healthy
-living/adult-health/expert-answers/how-many-hours-of-sleep-are-enough
/faq-20057898.

Pigeon, Wilfred, Carr, Michelle, Perlis, Michael. "Effects of a Tart Cherry Juice Beverage
on the Sleep of Older Adults with Insomnia: A Pilot Study." *Journal of Medicinal Food*
13, no. 3 (2010): 579–583. http://www.ncbi.nlm.nih.gov/pmc/articles/PMC3133468.

Schaeffer, Julian. "Spring Cleaning: Assessing the Benefits and Risks of Detox Diets." *Today's Dietitian*, May 2008, vol. 10, no. 5, p. 34. http://www.todaysdietitian.com /newarchives/tdmay2008pg34.shtml.

United States Department of Agriculture. National Nutrient Database. Accessed November 1, 2014. http://ndb.nal.usda.gov.

University of Maryland Medical Center. "Headaches." Accessed October 29, 2014. http://umm.edu/health/medical/reports/articles/headaches-tension.

Vitamix. Accessed November 4, 2014. https://www.vitamix.com/Shop/default.aspx? PROMO=103113-02&COUPON=07-0063&gclid=CPTPq_m28MECFYpgfgod RDoAMQ.

Wansink, Brian, and Sobal, Jeffrey. "Mindless Eating: The 200 Daily Food Decisions We Overlook." *Environment and Behavior* 39, no. 1 (January 2007): 106–123.

Whitney, Ellie, and Rolfes, Sharon. *Understanding Nutrition*. Thirteenth Edition. Boston: Wadsworth Cengage Learning, 2013.

The World's Healthiest Foods. Accessed November 1, 2014. http://www.whfoods.com.

RESOURCES

Calbom, Cherie. *The Ultimate Smoothie Book: 130 Delicious Recipes for Blender Drinks, Frozen Desserts, Shakes and More.* Grand Central Life & Style, June 2006.

Castle, Kirk. *100 Healthy Smoothie Recipes.* CreateSpace Independent Publishing Platform, January 2013.

Chace, Danielle. *More Smoothies for Life: Satisfy, Energize, and Heal Your Body.* Clarkson Potter, July 2007.

Daniels, Emma. *Vegan Smoothie Recipes: The Delicious, Weight Loss & Healthy Living Vegan Smoothie Recipe Book.* CreateSpace Publishing, May 2014.

Dobbins, Lee Anne. *Healthy Smoothie Recipes: Healthy Herbal Smoothies That Are Nutritious, Delicious and Easy to Make.* CreateSpace Independent Publishing Platform, May, 2012.

Joyner, Nadia. *Green Smoothies: 50+ Recipes for Nutrition, Life and Health.* CreateSpace Independent Publishing Platform, October, 2013.

Mendocino Press. *The Smoothie Recipe Book for Beginners: Essential Smoothies to Get Healthy, Lose Weight, Feel Great,* January 2014.

Morris, Julie. *Superfood Smoothies: 100 Delicious, Energizing & Nutrient Dense Recipes.* Sterling Publishing, May 2013.

Paul, Tamara. *Gluten-Free Smoothie Recipes.* CreateSpace Publishing, October 2014.

Roberts, Kasia, RN. *The Superfood Smoothie Recipe Book: Super-Nutritious, High-Protein Smoothies to Lose Weight, Boost Metabolism and Increase Energy.* CreateSpace Independent Publishing Platform, February 2014.

Rockridge Press. *The Smoothie Recipe Book: 150 Recipes Including Recipes for Weight Loss and Smoothies for Optimum Health* (Nook Book). Rockridge Press, 2013.

Rockridge University Press. *Green Smoothies for Beginners: Essentials to Get Started* (Nook Book). Rockridge University Press, Callisto Media, Inc. March 2013.

Sharpe, Diane. *The Fat Burner Smoothies: The Recipe Book of Fat Burning Superfood Smoothies for Weight Loss and Smoothies for Good Health.* CreateSpace Independent Publishing Platform, January 2014.

Sparks, Ariel. *Sugar-Free Green Smoothie Recipes.* CreateSpace Publishing, September 2014.

Swann-Miller, Liz. *The New Green Smoothie Diet Solution: Nature's Fast Lane to Peak Health.* CreateSpace Independent Publishing Platform, November 2012.

RECIPE INDEX

BENEFIT INDEX

INDEX

CPSIA information can be obtained at www.ICGtesting.com
Printed in the USA
BVOW10s0338160315

391690BV00005B/5/P